CHILDREN, CLAY
AND SCULPTURE

Children, Clay and Sculpture

Cathy Weisman Topal

Davis Publications, Inc.
Worcester, Massachusetts

Photographs by Marie Frank or Cathy Weisman Topal
unless otherwise noted. Line drawings by Cathy
Weisman Topal.

Cover: **Cellist,** David Aronson, 1969–1978. Clay
model, 14¼″ × 11½″ × 20¼″ (36.2 × 29.2 ×
51.4 cm). Courtesy Pucker/Safrai Gallery, Boston, Massachusetts. Photograph by Barney Burnstein.

This page: **Imaginary Beast,** Simone Topal, age 13.

Design: Blackbirch Graphics

Printed in the United States of America
Library of Congress Catalog Card Number: 83–71615
ISBN: 0-87192-145-6
10 9 8 7 6 5 4 3 2 1

Acknowledgements

Completion of this book required the help of
many people. My thanks go to Marie Frank for her
fine photography. Thanks also to Lynne Goldman
and Kay Lerner for their help in working out classroom activities, with special thanks to Kay for acting
as a sounding board and posing for photographs.

I am indebted to the administrators and teachers
who make the Smith College Campus School one
that encourages projects such as this book. The children in the school helped by testing the clay sculpture techniques. At Smith College, members of the
Department of Education and Child Study offered
welcome encouragement and suggestions. My
thanks go also to the museums, galleries, teachers
and artists who generously contributed photographs.

I am grateful to my parents, Charna and Phil
Weisman, and to my grandmother, Flora Slonim,
for nurturing my love of art and for taking care of
my family at critical moments. I thank my daugh-
ters, Simone, Rachel and Claire, and their friends;
they cheerfully tried out many of the activities explained here. Finally I wish to thank my husband,
Sam, for lovingly bearing with me throughout the
work on this book.

CONTENTS

INTRODUCTION

Clay sculpting comes naturally to children. With proper guidance, they can produce increasingly sophisticated clay sculpture. At the same time they can learn about and gain an appreciation of three-dimensional art.

This book provides teachers and parents with an easy way to guide children in this process. Many styles, methods, art principles and techniques are combined with advice on handling a group of youngsters, their clay and their enthusiasm.

Clay sculpture techniques are explained and then followed by step-by-step directions which summarize the techniques. These directions can be used independently by children as they work with clay. The directions lead students through the basics of a technique, yet invite creative solutions. Each section ends with a summary of the lesson's concepts, vocabulary and goals.

Throughout the book are brief discussions of three-dimensional art. Illustrations of finished sculptures by artists from many cultures, past and present, are also provided. The accompanying captions include information intended to extend the art appreciation lessons.

1

BEFORE YOU BEGIN

A ball of clay is all that is necessary to begin sculpting. Clay comes from the earth. It is usually found near water, around lakes, bays, riverbanks and creeks. Clay dries when it is exposed to air, but returns to a muddy state when it is placed in water. As a result it can be used again and again until it is **fired,** or baked in a kiln. A kiln is a special heat-resistant oven. The kiln reaches extremely high temperatures during firing. This fuses chemicals in the clay. After firing, the clay will not return to a muddy state but will hold water. See Appendix for information on obtaining clay.

A ball of clay is all you need to begin.

Moist balls of clay ready for classroom distribution.

Clay in the classroom

Clay can be one of the easiest art materials to use. It is self-contained. It can be used over and over again. No other supplies are essential, and children love it.

Many teachers associate clay with a big mess. Actually, the amount of mess is in direct proportion to the amount of water available. Water is the crucial variable. Refrain from introducing water until students have had experience with the clay. When water is introduced (see Chapter Two) treat its use as a skill to be mastered, and offer only a very small amount.

When planning to work with large groups of students, prepare the balls of clay ahead of time. The size of the ball depends on the size of the project and the size of the student's hands. Be certain that there are enough balls for each person in the group. Have many extra clay balls available in case a student's clay becomes too dry to work easily. Keep clay balls moist and portable by storing them in an airtight container such as a large, heavy-duty garbage bag closed with a wire twist.

Check the consistency of the clay a day before you want to use it. This can save countless last-minute frustrations.

Clay that is too dry cracks easily and is almost impossible to manipulate. If that is the condition of your clay, break it into pieces and place them in a plastic bag. Add some water and let the clay sit for a while. It will absorb the moisture. Then wedge it until it feels good (wedging instructions follow). Large lumps of clay may be wedged, divided and formed into smaller balls.

Clay that is too wet will stick to everything. It is discouraging to use and makes a mess. If that happens, put the clay on a large board and expose it to the air for a short time, turning it occasionally. Then wedge the clay until it feels good. If the room is hot and dry, don't leave the clay exposed to the air too long. It will dry out very quickly.

When clay is not being used, keep it covered with plastic to retain the moisture. Just add a sprinkling of water each time you put it away.

Individual work boards are invaluable. They absorb most of the mess and can be brushed or scraped after each use. They enable students to turn their sculptures around as they work, and to transport and store their projects. Discarded linoleum tiles or small pieces of cardboard, wood or Masonite all make excellent work boards. Boards that are a foot square are a good size for most projects.

Damp paper towels, one for each child, are a good alternative to individual work boards. They are convenient to use when traveling between classrooms. Damp paper towels make a good resting place for clay. They can also be used to clean hands and to wipe the table top when the session is over.

Before distributing clay to children, establish a few limitations. Two good rules are, "all clay stays in your hands or on the table" and "keep your messy hands to yourself." Children appreciate the humorous tone. If they forget these rules, they quickly lose the privilege of using clay for the rest of the period. That usually discourages potential troublemakers.

Clean-up can be simple and practically mud-free if all clay balls and tiny clay pieces are collected and all dried pieces scraped from work surfaces before sponging. Return clay to a plastic bag. Add some water before putting the clay away.

Just as all sculptors must practice and experiment before creating "works of art", many of the activities included in this book are exercises for practicing skills and techniques. The results are not meant to be saved. Students will need to know that there will be a time for them to save sculptures that are special. Begin by stressing practice and exploration, and by using clay again and again just for fun.

Preparing clay: wedging

Wedging is a basic part of clay preparation. This process gives the clay an even consistency. It also removes air bubbles, which expand under high heat. Air bubbles can cause clay sculptures to explode in the kiln, destroying themselves and ruining other pieces as well. For this reason, clay must be wedged if it is to be fired.

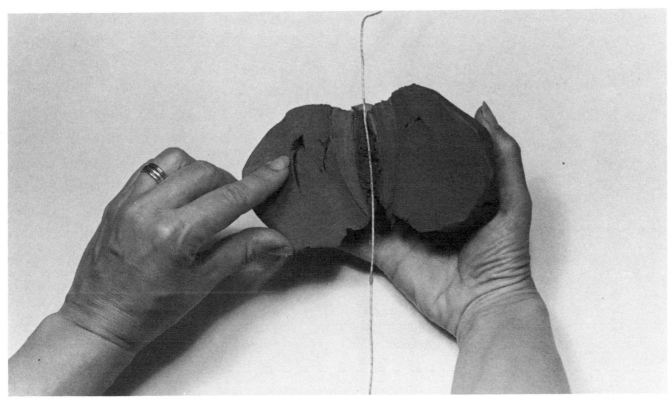

Air pockets like this one must be wedged out of the clay before making a piece that is to be fired.

Wedging takes additional time, and clay can become too dry to use when young children spend a long time wedging. For this reason many teachers prefer to wedge the clay themselves before distributing it to children. The reasons and techniques for wedging are intriguing and rewarding aspects of learning about clay, however, and are good for children to learn.

Wedging not only conditions the clay, but also sets the tone of a classroom. It enables children to become accustomed to an exciting new art medium and to feel the clay before beginning a more demanding project. Preparation of clay helps children ready themselves for more serious work.

The simplest wedging may be done by hitting a rounded piece of clay between both hands or by forcefully throwing clay onto a board. Young children can easily learn either method, and these usually are adequate for young children's work.

For the best results, have students use the more traditional wedging technique. The continued rocking and kneading motions lend calm to a classroom. Here is the standard wedging procedure:

Materials: Balls of clay, work boards, wire or string.

Directions:
1. Cut your clay in half with a string or wire to check for air bubbles.
2. Slap clay halves together with force to push out any air within the clay.
3. Knead your clay like bread. Rock clay forward. Punch down with the heels of your hands.
4. Continue rocking the clay forward and punching down for several minutes. You should develop a rhythm while you wedge. Your clay is ready for use when you can cut it anywhere and find no air bubbles.

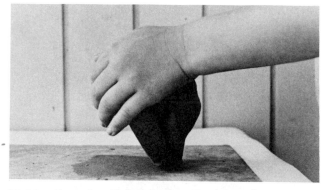

Wedging: Grasp clay with both hands, and rock forward.

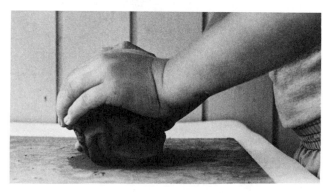

Wedging: Punch down with the heels of your hands to force out any trapped air bubbles.

Cutting clay: The two ends of the string or wire can be wrapped around small sticks to make them easier to grasp and use.

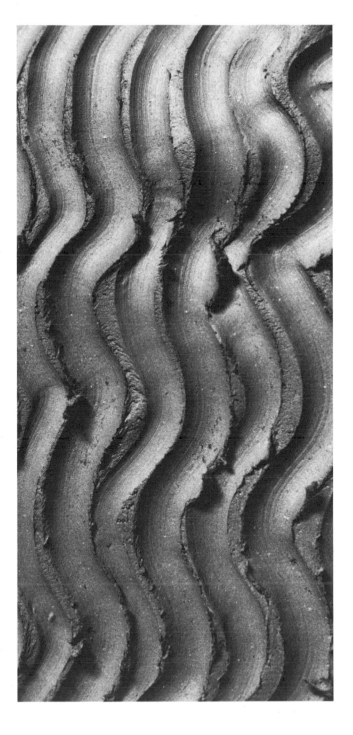

2

EXPLORATIONS

Hands are the only tools essential for clay exploration. Hands can change the form and texture of the clay in a matter of seconds. They can poke, pinch, pound, roll, squash, squeeze, stretch clay and much more. Working with clay fosters a special kind of communication among hands, clay and imagination. It is very personal, almost therapeutic experience.

Though it may look like a big lump, manipulation of clay often suggests familiar forms and situations to children. Children often respond to the suggested forms by making up stories and talking to themselves while they are working. Clay tools interfere with the wonderful communication that occurs when hands meet clay, so keep them out of sight for now.

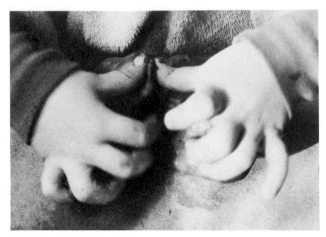

Pinching clay with thumbs.

Various muscles of the hands and fingers are called into play by exploratory exercises. Clay exercises encourage development of skill and muscle control. Any time you introduce a clay project, use one of these exercises as a starting point to warm up hands, clay and imaginations. Students of all ages need time to feel and manipulate the clay before going on to more demanding projects. After just a few minutes of clay exploration, they will be more focused and ready to work.

Demonstrate the activity, going through the directions step by step, talking about each step while manipulating the clay. Show, for example, that a ball of clay is a solid, three-dimensional form that occupies positive space. A **positive shape** is the solid part of a sculpture. Using fingers, thumbs and knuckles, demonstrate how easily one can open, change and enlarge the clay shape and the space around and inside it. Work slowly, commenting on the wonderful feel of the clay as it moves and stretches beneath your fingertips.

Poke a hole in the clay to demonstrate negative space. **Negative shapes** are the indentations and holes filled with air. You might even hold the clay under a strong light so that the forms in the sculpture cast shadows, dramatizing the negative and positive shapes. Turn the clay as you work. Point out the three dimensions of the form, and show the children that the clay looks different from each point of view.

Concentrate on the sturdiness of the form, the view from each angle and the surface texture. At the end, demonstrate that smoothing the entire clay shape is one way of finishing and unifying a sculpture.

After the demonstration, have students gather their supplies and begin to work. They can refer to the directions if they have forgotten a step.

The amount of clay distributed influences what students are able to do. Most exercises require a fist-size ball of clay. Smaller pieces give students more control when forming coils, balls, push pots and protuberances. Additional clay should always be available.

Exploratory exercises are not meant to be ends in themselves, although they could be used as such. The products are not meant to be kept, although they can be.

A three-year-old student rolls a coil, then stands it up to form a little arc.

Rolling coils between two hands.

Free exploration

Have students discover ways in which their hands or fingers can change the shape of the clay. Poking is one way, squeezing is another. There are many others.

Talk with children about their discoveries. This can make the exploratory process more meaning-ful. While circulating through the room, make comments that qualify and describe students' hand motions. For example, one child may use the side of his hand to pound his clay. The clay will show all the lines and details of his nails and fingers. Another student might use her knuckles to press small spaces into her clay, and push her thumbs upward to raise a little line from her ball of clay. Comments can encourage diversity and motivate students to try new approaches.

A **coil** is a long clay form that looks like a snake. Coiling is an ancient way of making large pots and sculptures. Coils can be long, thin, short or fat. They can be used in many ways to make designs. Have the children use coils to make a lit-tle person. They can put coils together to form the letters of their name. Encourage the children to try more than one way of using coils.

Questions encourage children to think and speak about their discoveries. For example, ask who can think of a way to make a very tall clay shape. There are many answers. Try to ask questions that challenge the children to extend what they are doing. Can they make it higher, flatter, longer, thinner? Can they poke any more space into the clay shape, or will it collapse?

A title for a clay shape can foster discussion of sculpture. A title yields more information and re-sponse than the question, "What is it?" which im-plies that it doesn't look like anything to you.

Comments, questions and titles extend explora-tion while they encourage students to develop a descriptive art vocabulary. They are applicable to all the activities in the book.

Shaking hands with clay

Directions:

1. Pat your clay into a large clay slab, or flat form, like a pancake. Cover your slab with thumbprints. Look closely.
2. Turn your slab over. Cover it with knuckle prints. Look closely. How do the knuckle prints differ from the thumbprints? In what ways are they similar?
3. Turn your slab over and make more prints, using fingers, sides of hands, fists, whole hands, elbows.
4. Look at a neighbor's clay. Guess which hand part made which impression.

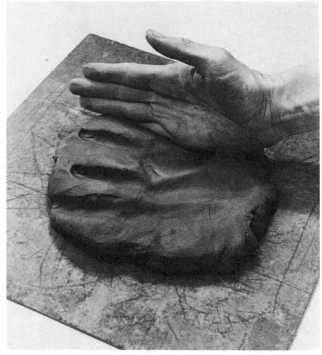

Impression from side of hand.

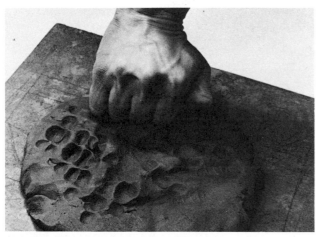

Knuckle impression.

Thumb impression.

Fist impression.

Before forming smaller details, push and poke very deep grooves, and pull and squeeze dramatically tall shapes.

Building up with clay

Material: A large lump of moist clay (about 25 pounds or 11 kilograms) for each small group of children. The students will work together on the clay, poking in and pulling out.

Directions:
1. Push, squeeze and shape your clay into a tall mountain range.
2. Use fingers, knuckles and thumbs to make textures, caves and tunnels.
3. Add to your mountain using other pieces of clay — on top, inside, underneath and so on.
4. Use some more clay to form the creatures that live in this mountain range.

Squeeze and sculpt

Directions:

1. In one hand, hold a ball of clay about the size of your fist.
2. With eyes closed, squeeze the clay until you get a form that has a variety of shapes: large and small, round and long, shallow and deep.
3. Open your eyes. Now poke, pull and model the shape until it pleases you when you look at it from many points of view. Be aware of the positive and negative shapes that you are creating. **Positive shapes** are the solid parts of a sculpture. **Negative shapes** are the areas or spaces around and between the solid forms. Negative shapes are filled with air.
4. Use your fingers to smooth the surface.

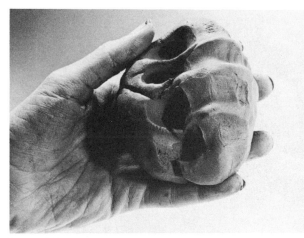

Squeezed shape.

Modeling a squeezed shape.

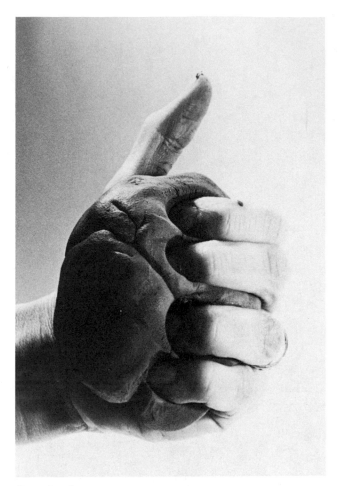

Squeezing clay.

When exploring clay it is fun and helpful to play games that expand awareness of other possibilities. For instance, each person could squeeze a shape and pass it to the person to the right. This person will use the shape to complete the exercise. Another game involves objects with unusual shapes such as pinecones, seed pods, shells, plastic bath toys or kitchen utensils. Put these into separate paper bags. Each child feels inside a bag and tries to model the shape he or she has felt, but not seen. After shapes are completed, bags can be opened and objects and shapes compared. The whole squeeze and sculpt activity can be done without looking, with clay and hands inside a brown bag. This is fun, too.

Basic techniques

The following explorations will be referred to again and again in the chapters that follow. Besides being useful for skills and acquaintance with clay, they are a lot of fun. They are well worth the time spent on them before beginning the later sculpture projects.

Rolling coils

Directions:

1. Break off a piece of clay about the size of a Ping-Pong ball. Put it on your work surface and roll it back and forth with one hand. Roll the clay back to the palms of your hands, then up to your fingertips. Keep your hands moving constantly.
2. When your coil is too big for one hand, use both hands together to roll the clay back and forth just as you did when you used only one hand. Concentrate on the fat places a bit more than on the skinny places. Try to roll a long, even coil.

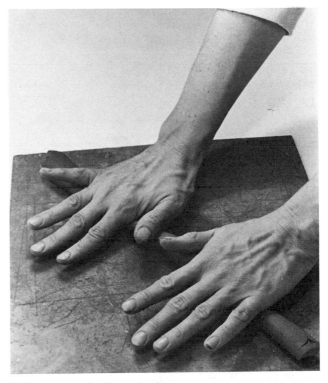

Rolling a long coil with two hands.

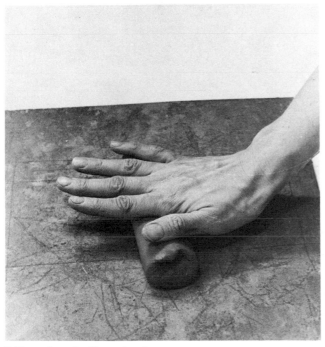

Rolling a fat coil with one hand.

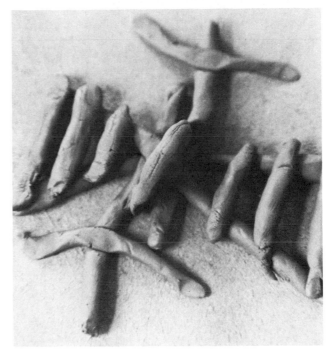

A symmetrical design in coils by Christopher Pennock, age 4.

3. If you don't move your hands while you roll, you will get an uneven coil. Experiment by changing the placement and pressure of your hands as you roll. Uneven coils make very interesting and unusual forms.
4. Make coils that are skinny, fat, short or long. Use your coils to make squiggles, spirals and zig-zags.
5. Join your coils in some way. Make a design. Make numbers and letters. Overlap the coils and stand them up on their ends. Try making roads, bridges, people, animals and trees.

The animal form in this belt plaque suggests some of the very sophisticated designs that can be made by joining simple coiled forms. **Belt Plaque**, *Caucasian, 5th–3rd century* B.C., *Bronze, 3″ × 3½″ (7.5 × 9 cm). Courtesy Mead Art Museum, Amherst College, Amherst, Massachusetts.*

Making a coil sculpture.

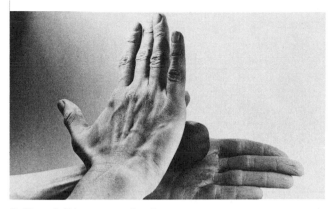

Rolling a ball between two hands.

Rolling balls

A ball is a round clay form. The motions used to make a ball are different from those used to make a coil.

Directions:
1. Break your lump of clay into several pieces of different sizes. Try rolling balls in two ways: between your hands or with one hand on the table. Which way is easier for you? Make balls of many different sizes.
2. Try putting your balls together. What can you make?

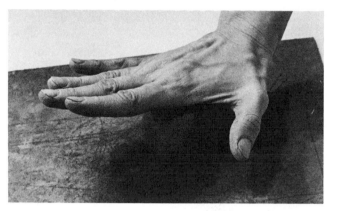

Rolling a ball on the table.

Clay ball sculpture by Justin Sacks, age 3.

Making a sculpture from clay balls of different sizes.

Hold a ball of clay.

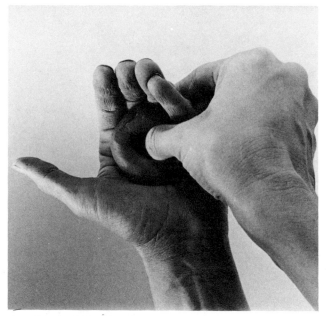

Press down with your thumb.

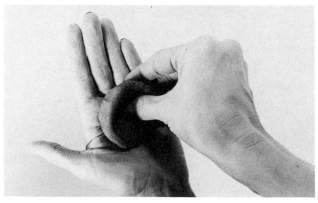

Push and turn.

Push pots

A push pot is an open clay form or bowl that is made by holding a clay ball in the hands and shaping it with fingers and thumbs. Push pots often are called pinch pots. The word "pinch" implies using much more pressure than is desirable. "Push" seems to be a more accurate description of the kind of pressure and motion used in creating a successful pot. It is harder to make push pots than it looks. It takes practice. Prepare two or three Ping-Pong ball size clay balls beforehand for each student.

Directions:
1. Hold a small ball of clay in the palm of one hand.
2. Push a hole into the center of your clay ball with the thumb or finger from your other hand. Don't push it in too far, or you will make a hole all the way through your clay. If you do

Continue to open the pot.

The palm of the maker's hand gives the shape of the finished pot.

go through your clay, push the clay back to cover the hole, or start again.

3. Turn the clay with the fingers of one hand as you push against the palm of your other hand. Your palm acts as support for the clay. Work to this rhythm: push and turn and push and turn and push and turn. You are trying to enlarge the size of the pot by stretching out the walls and bottom of your clay form. If you continue pushing and turning at a steady rate, the sides of your pot should be even. It takes practice, so try several balls.

4. Push the bottom of the pot against a flat surface to make it stand.

5. Try making pots from ovals as well as from circles. Try using different fingers to form different sized and shaped pots. Try thumb pots, pinky pots, elbow pots and pointer pots.

6. Put all of your pots together and join them by pressing and smoothing.

A finger pot that was shaped around an index finger.

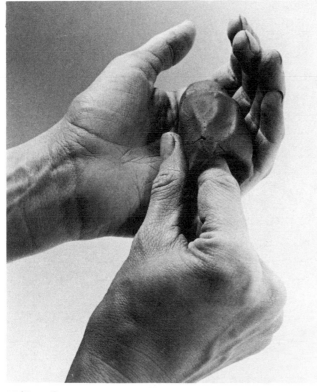

Making a finger pot.

Push pots combined.

Breaking and rejoining clay

Directions:

1. Break your clay into many small pieces. How many can you count?
2. How can you arrange them? Try lining them up, piling them and putting them in a circle.
3. Find a way to attach all the pieces, such as pressing and smoothing.

Smoothing clay with water

Directions:

1. Make a clay shape that pleases you, using any of the preceding techniques.
2. Before using any water, try smoothing your shape all over with your fingertips. Often water is unnecessary.
3. Now, dip your fingertips into water, and gently rub them over the surface of the clay. Smooth the whole sculpture until it is no longer shiny from the added water. Do not use too much water or your sculpture will become muddy.

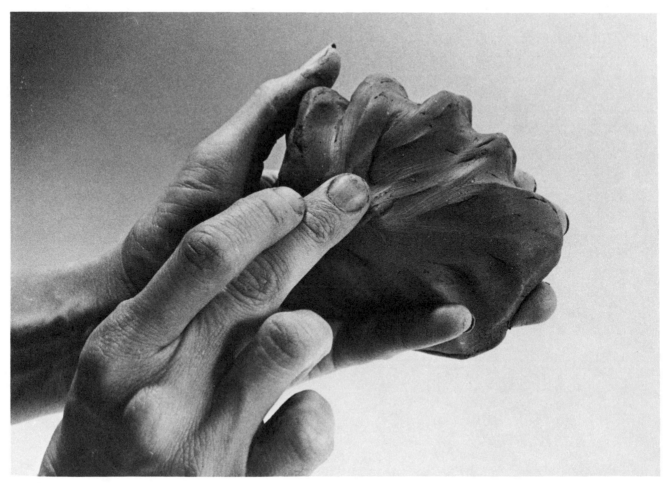

Smoothing.

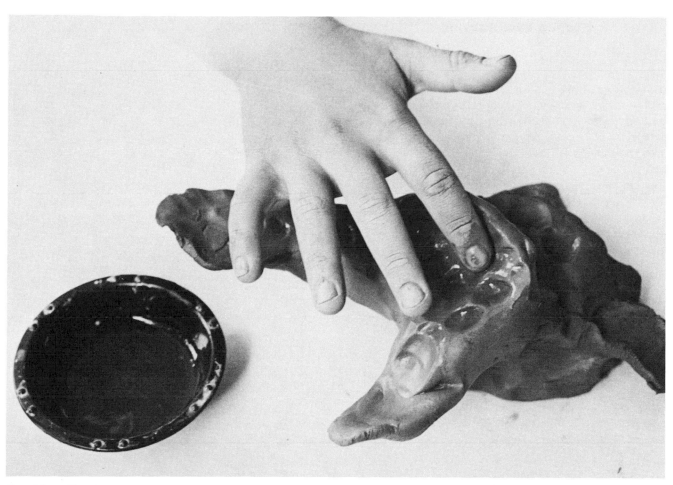

Smoothing with water.

Students may need a chance to discover what happens when too much water is used. A small, moist sponge for each student can supply enough water to smooth and moisten dry clay, making water dishes unnecessary. Small squares of sponge may be cut from a larger kitchen sponge.

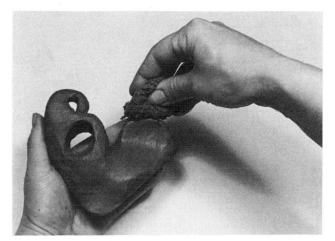

Smoothing with a sponge.

Group explorations

Clay shapes from any of the preceding exercises may be combined to make group sculptures. This is one more way to add a new dimension to an exploratory clay session. To combine clay shapes, students must look at their artwork from a new perspective. They must search for the best way and place to make a connection between their work and the work of their neighbor. Students should consider several possibilities before pressing and smoothing their clay shapes together. If clay forms are to be squashed and put away for another day, students sometimes find this easier if they can end the session with a group composition.

Summary of clay exploration concepts

Initial practice should help children learn techniques for **pulling, pushing, poking, rolling, pressing, stretching** and **smoothing** clay. They should learn to roll balls and **coils** (even and uneven), shape **push pots** and smooth using a little water. While discovering how to connect clay shapes and make group sculptures, children can learn to share ideas and work together.

3

MAKING SCULPTURE

Sculptures, like all great works of art, can speak across large spans of time and across language barriers to the eyes, mind and soul of the viewers. They communicate the visions of the artists who created them, and cause us, the viewers, to perceive something about the world in a new or different way.

The words *realistic*, *abstract* and *nonobjective* are used to describe and categorize sculptures. **Realistic** refers to the degree to which a form imitates nature, or is true to life. One sculpture may be more realistic or abstract than another. Of the three sculptures pictured on the following pages, *Seated K'uan-Yin* (page 31) is the most realistic.

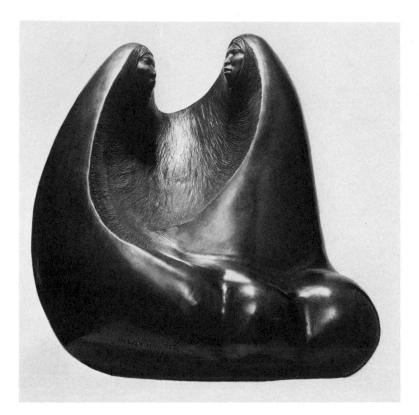

In this sculpture, our eyes are drawn to the very detailed, expressive and realistic faces of the two Indian women. The swirling, textured area draws our attention to the faces again and again. Only later do we notice that the rest of the sculpture is abstract. We can sense the calm and spiritual closeness of these two women, and we wonder what they are talking and thinking about. **Camp Talk,** Allan Houser. *Bronze, 8th edition, 23½″ × 22½″ × 21½″ (59.5 × 57.1 × 54.6 cm). Courtesy The Gallery Wall, Scottsdale, Arizona. Photograph by Abrams Photo/graphics.*

Abstract sculptures are based on realistic forms, but do not look real. By exaggerating, distorting, simplifying or geometrizing, artists express their feelings, impressions or reactions to realistic forms. Abstract sculptures focus our attention on position, action, character or expression. This forces us to confront a different level of reality. Abstract sculptures often convey information by using very few details.

A **nonobjective** sculpture doesn't represent a recognizable object. When artists create nonobjective sculptures, they choose to work with forms and relationships in space. The artists are not representing or recreating reality. *Cubi VII* by David Smith and *Sculptural Object* by Henry Moore are nonobjective sculptures.

Sculpting is the art of creating forms and arranging them in space. When we look at a mass of clay as a sculpture, we have gone a step beyond manipulation and exploration. We have shifted our focus from the motions of hands to the form of clay as it occupies space.

There are two basic kinds of forms, geometric and organic. **Geometric forms,** such as cones, cubes, spheres, pyramids and cylinders, are precise and regular. They suggest human-made objects such as buildings, tables and boxes. **Organic forms,** such as forms in nature, suggest growth and movement. Organic forms often are irregular and curvilinear.

Sculpture has positive and negative shapes (see Chapter Two). Sculptural forms invite viewers to become involved by moving around and sometimes inside the sculpture. Viewers discover new forms, spaces, relationships and surfaces with each step or tilt of the head.

Though they may not intend to, children often make sculptures that look more abstract or nonobjective than realistic. Teachers can capitalize on this tendency. A nonobjective or abstract approach to sculpture may be used from the beginning. This has many advantages. It encourages beginning students to focus on basic art concepts of shape, form, space and texture, and on art principles of repetition, balance, contrast and variety. Students are freer to explore the potential of clay as a sculptural medium. They grow accustomed to using an art vocabulary and to viewing their work from a formal standpoint. They can then apply their skills and knowledge to the creation of realistic works if they choose.

Modeling a clay ball, sculpting a slab and consideration of composition and texture offer different ways to approach clay sculpting. Each approach is explained here with suggested clay activities.

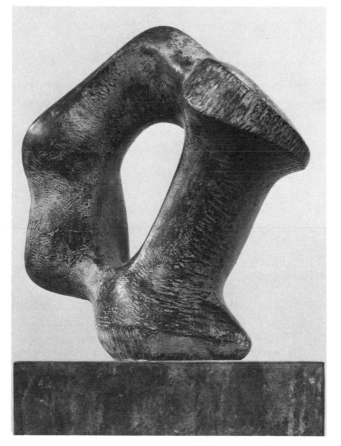

A sculpture exists in space. It can be seen from many points of view and against a variety of backgrounds. The size of a sculpture is important too. *Sculptural Object* is much smaller than *Cubi XII*. This sculpture is organic. It suggests natural forms such as bones or the knots of an old tree trunk. **Sculptural Object**, Henry Moore, 1960. *Bronze, 28¾" (73 cm). Courtesy Smith College Museum of Art, Northampton, Massachusetts. Anonymous gift of friends in memory of Louise Lindner Eastman '33, 1962.*

By treating the sculptural medium in various ways, artists cause light, shadow and reflections to play across a sculpture's surface. David Smith used a swirling motion to polish the welded steel cubes and rectangles within Cubi XII. The form of the sculpture contrasts with its surface texture. **Cubi XII**, David Smith, 1963. *Stainless steel, 109⅝" × 49¼" × 32¼" (278.5 × 125.1 × 81.9 cm). Courtesy Hirshhorn Museum and Sculpture Garden, Smithsonian Institution. © Estate of David Smith.*

Features and details here are entirely eliminated. Appendages are almost geometric forms, positioned to suggest a figure. Even the guitar is made of highly stylized geometric shapes. This sculpture might be mistaken for a nonobjective sculpture, if it were not for the title. **Reclining Nude with Guitar,** Jacques Lipchitz, 1928. *Bronze, 16⅛″ × 29⅝″ × 12¾″ (41.1 × 75.3 × 32.2 cm). Courtesy Hirshhorn Museum and Sculpture Garden, Smithsonian Institution, Washington, D.C.*

K'uan-Yin, Goddess of Mercy, is dressed in an elegant robe which gently conforms to the curves of her body. Her proportions, position and features are very natural, and appear true to life. Notice the fine details of her face, hair, fingers, toes and jewelry. **Seated K'uan-Yin,** *artist unknown, Chinese, 18th century(?). White porcelain, 3¾″ × 2½″ × 1⅝″ (9.5 × 6.4 × 4.2 cm). Collection of Mount Holyoke College Art Museum, South Hadley, Massachusetts. Gift of the estate of Jennie Tower, 1944. Photography by David Stansbury.*

Modeling

Poking and pulling are two basic modeling techniques. Space can be poked into a clay ball, or protuberances can be pulled. **Protuberances** are parts that extend from the main body of a sculpture. Holes and protuberances involve a clay mass in its surrounding space.

Opening a solid

Realistic or abstract two-dimensional works, such as drawings, paintings or photographs, are illusions of objects such as houses, trees and people. Viewing these, we can see the objects, but we cannot grasp them or walk around them. We can also see the space or air surrounding the objects, but we cannot step into it or wave our arms around in it. That is because a two-dimensional work is flat. The medium has only length and width, though the image *appears* to have depth.

A three-dimensional work of art has length, width and measurable depth. We can touch the solid alabaster stone of *Figure in a Landscape*. We can run our hands over its smooth surface. We can walk in the space that surrounds it and look through it to the other side. When artists make sculptures, works of art that are three-dimensional, they create objects, not pictures of objects. The experience is very different from working on a flat surface.

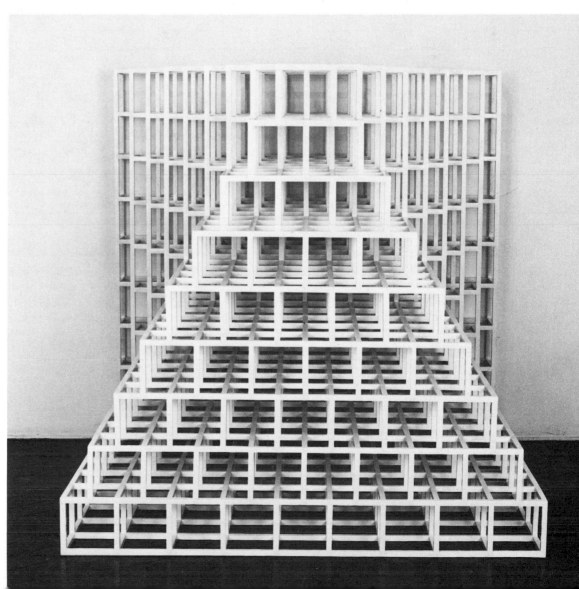

Contrast the open geometric forms in this sculpture with the solid geometric shapes in *Cubi XII* by David Smith. Notice the proportions of negative and positive shapes in each sculpture. Lewitt's sculpture seems much lighter than Smith's because it contains a large amount of negative space. **Cube Structure Based on Nine Modules,** Sol Lewitt, 1967–77. *Painted birch, 43″ × 43″ × 43″ (109.2 × 109.2 × 109.2 cm). Courtesy Smith College Museum of Art, Northampton, Massachusetts.*

The translucency of alabaster is an important element in the statement of this sculpture. Artists who make sculptures from stone use the subtractive process. Pieces of stone are carved away, or subtracted, as the artist works. The resulting sculpture depends not only on the artist's ideas and skills, but also on the nature of the medium that is sculpted. **Figure in a Landscape (trencrom),** Barbara Hepworth, 1952. *Alabaster, 5¼" × 10" (13.3 × 25.3 cm). Courtesy Smith College Museum of Art, Northampton, Massachusetts.*

Barbara Hepworth began *Figure in a Landscape* by looking at a solid piece of stone. She must have walked around it, studying it from different positions or **points of view.** She probably ran her hands over the stone, feeling the **texture,** the quality of its surface. Finally she began carving into the stone, changing its form with each cut. Little by little, she opened up the solid form, allowing the surrounding space to flow into, around and through the once-solid stone. The terms **form** and **mass** are used to describe a shape that has three dimensions, though the term **shape** may be used as well.

Notice the two rounded holes or spaces in the sculpture. They are very important to the sculpture, even though there is nothing there but air. Spaces such as these are negative shapes (see Chapter Two). The actual stone is a positive shape. It occupies positive space. Both positive and negative shapes are important to the overall effect of a sculpture.

Unlike *Figure in a Landscape*, there are no dramatic negative shapes in *Orient Shadow*, at least not when we look at it from this point of view. Perhaps because of that, the depth, shape and size of each indentation become more noticeable and important. The sculpture seems to undulate as light and shadow play over its highly-polished curves.

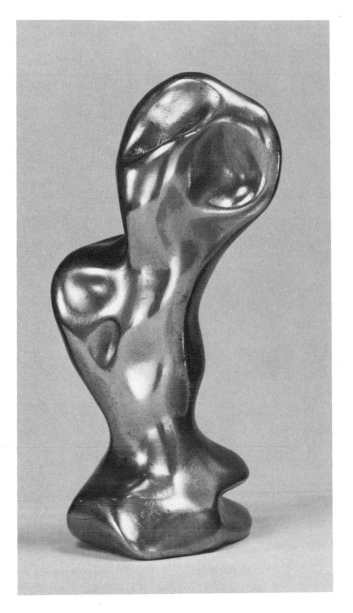

To make the clay model for this sculpture, Jean Arp probably began with a solid mass of clay. He may have pressed his thumbs and fingers gently into the malleable clay, rotating it in his hands as he worked. He must have noted the ever-changing form of the clay as he strove to get the right balance of big and small shapes and deep and shallow spaces.

Have children look for differences and similarities between these two sculptures. This is an excellent way to begin a class discussion. One obvious similarity is that both are nonobjective. They don't look like the objects that we see in our world. When the visual examples used during discussions are nonobjective, it is easier to understand concepts such as space and mass. Instead of using words such as *person*, *house* or *tree*, the class will need to use terms such as *form*, *mass*, *curved shape*, *deep space* and *negative shape*.

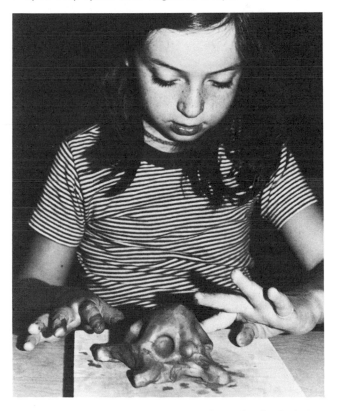

Creating a sculpture by poking in. Because this student has looked at a variety of nonobjective sculptures by noted artists, she can see her own work from a more professional and serious point of view.

To make a sculpture of metal an artist can begin with a clay model. Plaster is applied to all wet clay surfaces. When the plaster has hardened, it is carved in half, the wet clay model is removed, and the plaster halves are rejoined. This creates a hollow mold of the original clay model. Hot liquid metal is then poured into the hollow space and allowed to harden. When the plaster is removed, a metal sculpture remains, with the form of the original. The sculptor often smooths and polishes the surface to achieve a high gloss. **Orient Shadow (Ombre d'Orient),** *Jean (Hans) Arp, 1961. Bronze, 5⅜″ × 2¹⁵⁄₁₆″ × 2⅜″ (13.2 × 7.5 × 6.1 cm). Courtesy Smith College Museum of Art, Northampton, Massachusetts. Gift of the Estate of Mrs. Sigmund W. Kunstadter (Maxine Weil '24), 1978.*

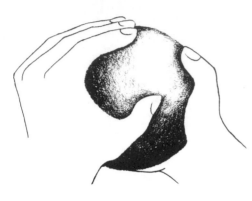

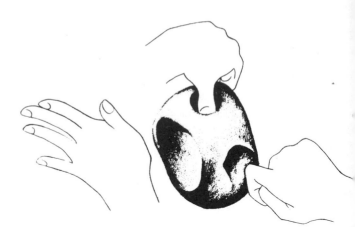

Poke in with different hand parts.

Opening a solid

Have the children make a sculpture by letting space into their clay. They should use different parts of their hands and fingers as they press, poke and open up a solid ball of clay. Suggest that they work slowly and thoughtfully with slow, smooth movements. They can use their eyes and sense of touch as a guide. Have the students keep the clay in their hands and turn it often.

Materials: Fist-size balls of clay, soft, malleable but not sticky.

Directions:

1. Pat your clay into a ball.
2. Gently use fingers, thumbs, knuckles, palms, and fists to poke and press openings in your clay. Make the openings differ in size and shape.
3. Poke some openings all the way through your clay.
4. Gently press some deep and shallow spaces, too.
5. Continue poking and pressing into your clay until you are pleased with the shape of your sculpture and with the way it uses space. Is your sculpture interesting from all points of view? Which point of view do you like best? Why? Where are the negative shapes? Where are the positive shapes? Give your sculpture a title.
6. If you do not like the shape of your clay, add to it, or roll it up and begin again. If your clay is very dry, get a fresh ball. Remember that you are experimenting.
7. When you are finished, gently smooth the entire surface with your thumbs and fingertips. This gives a feeling of unity to your clay form.

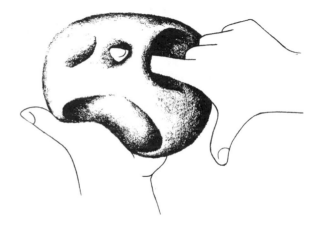

Poke some places all the way through.

Press some shallow spaces, too.

Pulling protuberances

The following exercise leads to creation of clay forms with sturdy, protruding parts. This is more difficult than the poking exercise, especially for younger children. Circulate around the room as children work. To spot those children who need help, ask them to model a sturdy part in clay and hold it up. Note that the term *model* is used here rather than the word *pinch*, which implies using too much pressure. Have the children create a sculpture by pulling small and large protuberances.

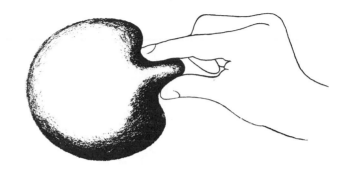

Model a small protuberance.

Directions:
1. Wedge clay (see Chapter One).
2. Use your first finger and your thumb to pull some small "outs" or protuberances. Make each part sturdy by going around it lightly several times with your finger and thumb.
3. Use all of your fingers and your thumb to pull a large protuberance from another area of your clay. Pull and press with your fingers and your thumb just a little bit at a time. Let the clay stretch out gradually or you may pull pieces off. Again, reinforce and smooth the protuberance by going around it many times.
4. Continue pulling small and large "outs" or protuberances until the clay and space form interesting negative and positive shapes.
5. Smooth the finished sculpture.
6. Give your sculpture a title.

Pull a large protuberance.

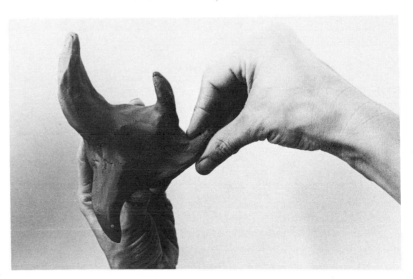

Modeling and pulling protuberances.

Solitary figures marching to an unknown destination recur in this sculptor's art. In this piece, slab pathways seem to curve and spiral endlessly in space, suggesting themes of time, life, death and heaven. The artist evokes feelings in us as we think about the people in this sculpture and wonder where they are going. **Cosmic Orbits**, Mirtala Bentov. *Bronze, 11½" (29.2 cm). Courtesy Pucker/Safrai Gallery, Boston, Massachusetts.*

This piece illustrates all of the criteria for sculpting sturdy parts. Student sculptures sometimes resemble primitive sculptures such as this. Art works from cultures all over the world can open students' eyes and build their confidence. **Seated Female Figure**, *Mexican, Tarascan from Nayarit, circa 300–700* A.D. *Terra cotta with incised details and traces of paint, 7½" × 5" (19 × 12.7 cm). Courtesy Smith College Museum of Art, Northampton, Massachusetts. Gift of Dr. and Mrs. Malcolm W. Bick.*

What makes a sculpture sturdy?

Fragile, protruding parts seem to cause many problems in sculpting with clay. It is a good idea to build skills early. After the children try the preceding exercises, go over the criteria for a sturdy part. A sturdy part:
- is firmly attached to the main sculpture.
- supports itself or the sculpture.
- is usually widest where it joins the main body of the sculpture.
- may need to be made shorter or fatter than it is in "real life."

- sometimes is connected to the sculpture in more than one place.

Have students look at a few sculptures to notice the ways in which other sculptors have made their clay forms sturdy. Then encourage them to use one or more of the techniques on their own sculptures. Reinforcing techniques not only make a sculpture sturdy, but they often make the positive and negative shapes more interesting. These techniques apply to all sculpture activities in the book. They are especially helpful to use later as a reference when sculpting figures or animals.

Connections between forms balance and reinforce a sculpture. They also contribute to its impact, indicating relationships between forms and figures. Forms that touch seem to be related. Forms that are separate may seem lonely. Notice the beautiful negative shapes produced by the connecting forms in this Eskimo sculpture. **Man and Woman,** Peter Egyitchiak. *Soapstone. Courtesy Pucker/Safrai Gallery, Boston, Massachusetts. Photograph by George Vasquez.*

Adding clay and joining parts

Children are proud of the many small details that they can form out of clay and push onto the main sculpture. Additions can be made when the clay is moist and the pieces can be firmly pressed and smoothed onto the clay. Unfortunately, as a clay piece dries those small pieces dry first and tend to fall off. Sooner or later a teacher will need to show students how to add extra clay pieces so that they will hold. This is especially important if the sculpture is to be fired. Following are two methods for adding clay parts.

Mirtala Bentov is a contemporary artist and poet. Her sculpture, like poetry, causes us to look beyond everyday events to the spiritual part of life. Here she deliberately uses only the essentials of the figure to suggest a relationship. **Twin Souls,** Mirtala Bentov. *Bronze, 6½"* *(16.5 cm). Courtesy Pucker/Safrai Gallery, Boston, Massachusetts.*

Adding by pressing and smoothing This technique works well when the clay is moist and workable. One difficulty with this technique is that it does take a few minutes. Often students are in a hurry. When they see how to add clay and understand why the clay needs to be firmly attached, they will be more willing to take the time. Students can make a game of checking each other's sculptures to see if they can find the places where the clay pieces were joined.

Smoothing to add moist clay.

Directions:

1. Press extra clay onto your sculpture. To add sculptural parts, such as legs or arms, poke a small hole where the new part will go. Then insert the end of the addition. Be careful not to let air bubbles form when attaching pieces.
2. Press and smooth the two pieces together using your thumbs and fingers. Smooth the clay all around the added part. Take your time and work carefully. When you finish smoothing you should not be able to see where the clay was joined.
3. Continue your sculpture.

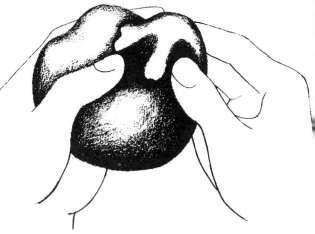

Attaching a clay part by placing it in a hole.

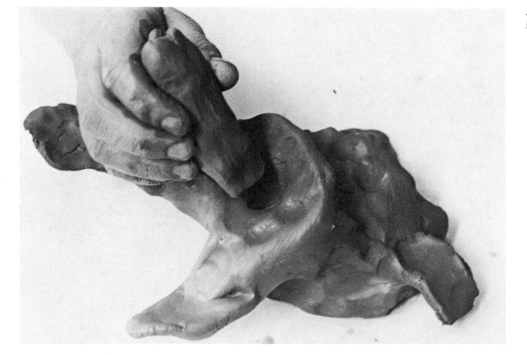

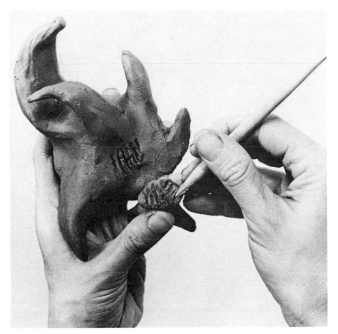

Rough up two surfaces.

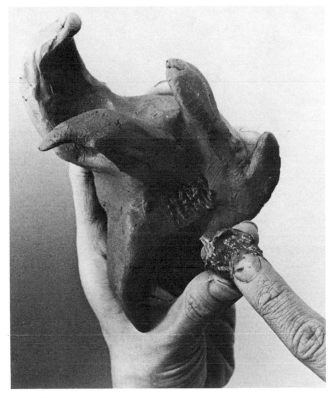

Apply slip.

Scoring Scoring is the safest way to join two parts together. When joining detailed, sculptured parts, such as heads or appendages, this usually is the technique to use. When joining clay pieces that have dried to the leather hard stage, they must be scored or the parts will not hold together. **Leather hard** clay feels cool and moist but is hard enough to hold its shape. Runny clay, or **slip,** is spread between two roughened clay surfaces, acting as glue to knit the two parts together. Pressing and smoothing should be done with extra care.

Materials: Slip (clay watered down to pea soup consistency), and a fork, pointed stick or pencil.

Directions:
1. Use a fork, pointed stick or pencil to "rough-up" or scratch the two surfaces to be joined.
2. Apply slip to one side.
3. Press the two pieces together firmly.
4. Use your fingers, clay tool, or both to smooth the two pieces together until you cannot tell where the pieces have been joined.
5. Continue your sculpture.

Press the pieces together.

Smooth the juncture.

A shape comes to life

This modeling activity taps student imaginations while it combines poking and pulling skills. It often yields striking results. Clay shapes turn into forms that suggest primitive and abstract sculpture.

Directions:

1. Wedge clay and pat it into a ball. Poke in and poke through in one or two places.
2. Pull some small and large protuberances.
3. Poke, pull and turn your clay until its form suggests something to you, perhaps an animal or a person.
4. Add any parts needed to make your suggested form come to life. Be sure that each part is sturdy. Smooth the sculpture if you choose.
5. If you don't like the results, squash your clay and begin again with a fresh, moist ball.
6. Give your sculpture a title.

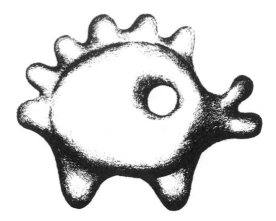

Turn it into an abstract sculpture.

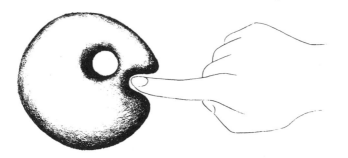

Poke in and through.

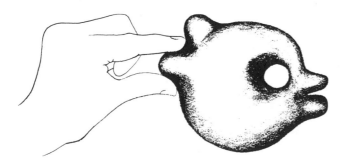

Pull out.

This is a large sculpture. Its gleaming black surfaces and protuberances suggest many feelings and images. *Lunar Bird* is at once imposing, scary and delightful. Students are particularly responsive to Miro's work because it is humorous, sophisticated yet childlike. Space creatures are a popular theme for young children. **Lunar Bird,** Joan Miro, 1966. *Bronze, 90⅛″ × 81¼″ × 59⅛″ (228.9 × 206.4 × 150.2 cm). Courtesy Hirshhorn Museum and Sculpture Garden, Smithsonian Institution, Washington, D.C. © by ADAGP, Paris, France, 1983.*

Summary of modeling concepts

Modeling is basic to understanding sculpture and the rest of the activities in this book. Though the exercises are fairly simple, the accompanying concepts usually are quite new to students (concepts such as **two-dimensional, three-dimensional, form, mass, space, positive and negative shapes, realistic, abstract, nonobjective** and **point of view**). List the terms in a visible place and encourage students to use them. If students have to use one or more terms to share ideas with the rest of the class, they will gradually incorporate the terms and concepts into their vocabulary.

It is not easy to master the skills involved in modeling parts, adding on parts and making a sculpture. They require practice. Experimental practice gives students many opportunities to fail and to succeed in an expected and accepted way. The outcome is not as crucial as it will be later when they model the parts for a realistic sculpture.

In this slab sculpture, the artist has explored clay with texture, color and shape. Emphasis is on the facial form. The rough free-form edges of the slabs in this sculpture contribute to the overall effect. **Rafaga,** Susana Espinosa, 1980. *Construction with clay strips, oxide stain, engobes, 16″ × 17″ × 2″ (40.6 × 43.2 × 5.1 cm). Courtesy of the artist. Photograph by Jochi Melero.*

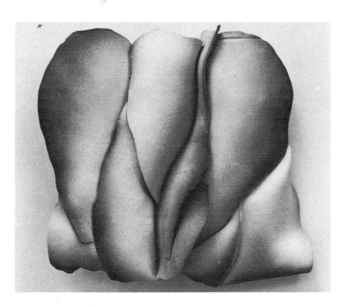

The thin, delicate, curving slab forms of this sculpture suggest some ways wind and water might shape crevices, hills and valleys in the desert. Subtle acrylic washes dramatize and accentuate each curve and undulation. **New Mexico,** Diane Kaiser, 1978. *Fired clay/acrylic, 11″ × 13″ × 3″ (27.9 × 33 × 7.6 cm). Collection of Ms. Joan Watts, Wilton, Connecticut. Photograph by the artist.*

Slab sculpture

A **slab** is a large, flat piece of clay. The slab method of sculpting allows a dramatically different approach to creating sculpture. It is the quickest way to create a large sculptural form. Instead of poking space into a form or pulling protuberances from a form, slabs enable the sculptor to shape space by wrapping it, as well as by dividing it with clay walls. There are two ways to make a slab: rolling and throwing.

The viewer can almost feel water moving back and forth around these curved forms. Their similarity makes the subtle variations more dramatic. Though sculpted from clay, they do not seem hard or static. The artist placed these forms on the floor at intervals, so that the viewer can walk among them. It is unusual to look down and around to see a sculpture, rather than viewing it at eye level. **Sea Garden,** Diane Kaiser, 1975. *Terra cotta, 120″ × 12″ × 168″ (305 × 30.5 × 427 cm). Photograph courtesy of the artist.*

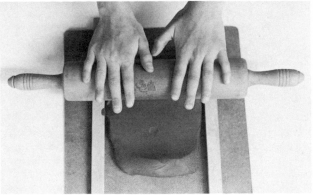

Rolling a slab.

Rolling a slab

Rolling is a reliable way to get a slab of uniform thickness.

Materials: Clay, work boards, sticks about 12 inches long and ¾ inch thick (30 by 2 centimeters), rolling pin or wooden dowel.

Directions:
1. Wedge some clay and shape it into a ball. Flatten it by pressing and patting until it is about as large as your hand and thicker than the sticks. Place the clay on a board or a piece of newspaper. On either side of the clay, place two sticks of even thickness (about ¾ inch or 2 centimeters. Sticks are not necessary, but they help. If newspaper is used, replace it if it gets too wet.
2. Place the rolling pin on top of the sticks and roll it back and forth along the entire length of the clay. Turn the clay around and over after every few rolls, so that it does not stick to the board or work surface. Stand up while rolling a slab. This enables you to use the weight of your body for added pressure.
3. If a textured slab is desired, roll the clay on a piece of textured cloth such as burlap.

Detail, **Sea Garden**.

Throwing a slab.

Throwing a slab

Some practice is required to throw a slab. Once the technique is learned, however, throwing clay slabs becomes a very satisfying experience. Throwing enables the sculptor to watch and feel the clay stretch, and to truly appreciate the elasticity of the medium. Teachers must be cautioned to try throwing only with a well-disciplined class!

Directions:

1. Wedge some clay and shape it into a ball. Flatten it by pressing and patting until it is almost as large as your hand. Place the flattened clay on a board or work surface.
2. Lift the far side of the clay slab with your fingertips. Without letting go, pull the far edge toward you with a decisive, steady motion. At the same time throw the clay down on the table. This will stretch the clay. As in rolling, it is almost impossible to do this while seated.
3. Repeat this process, turning the slab each time, until you get a slab of the desired thickness. Once you get the feel of throwing, you can make the slabs stretch in a desired manner.

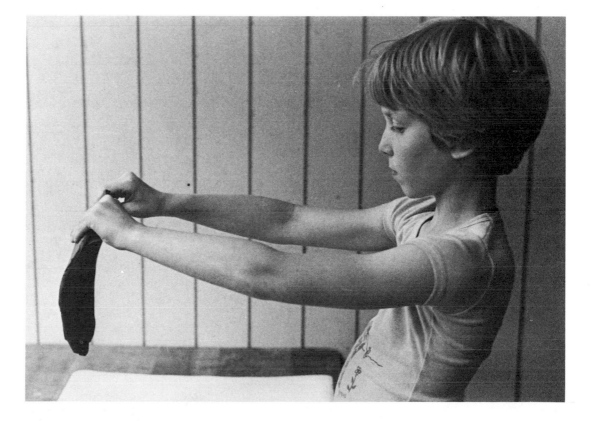

Shaping slabs

A slab may be varied by changing its thickness, size and texture. It may also be shaped in a variety of ways. By lifting, bending, folding or twisting, many **organic** shapes, shapes that resemble parts of living organisms, may be created. A slab can be draped over an **armature,** or support structure, to create an organic or free-form shape. Crushed newspapers, cardboard boxes and tubing from paper towels all make excellent armatures. Precise geometric shapes can be created by wrapping clay slabs around newspaper-covered cardboard shapes. The newspaper wrapping makes it easy to remove the cardboard shapes once the clay is hard enough to hold the shape by itself.

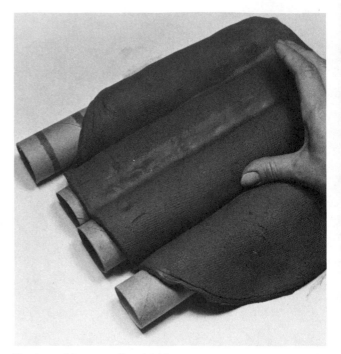

Draping a slab over cardboard tubing.

Geometric clay forms may be created by wrapping clay slabs around solid forms or by assembling previously-cut parts. The artist then faces the challenge of altering the regular form. **Tejido,** Susana Espinosa, 1979. *Clay slabs and coils, engobes (clay slip), oxide stain, 27″ × 12″ × 4″ (68.6 × 30.5 × 10.2 cm). Collection of Mrs. Rosario Ferrer de Aguilar, Puerto Rico. Courtesy of the artist. Photograph by Jochi Melero.*

When the clay forms have hardened enough to hold their shapes, yet still are cool and moist to the touch, they are in the **leather hard** stage of drying. Clay shrinks as it hardens. It is important to remove the armature from the clay when it is leather hard, to prevent it from cracking as it shrinks. To do this, a clay form can be cut in half, the armature removed and the pieces reassembled by scoring. If crushed newspaper is used for support inside a slab form, do not worry about any paper that cannot be easily removed from the form. The clay can shrink around loosely-packed newspaper without cracking. The leftover paper will burn out in the kiln if the piece is fired. This will leave a few ashes and a black residue.

During firing, hollow clay shapes act as giant air bubbles and can explode. If the piece is to be fired and it doesn't already have an opening, a hole should be poked through to the hollow space before the clay hardens. Hot air will escape through the opening while the sculpture is in the kiln. This will prevent the piece from exploding and ruining other sculptures in the kiln.

These figures were developed from a clay cylinder which was textured, colored and fairly wet. They were then "seated" in a loose way. Heads and details were attached to the cylindrical form. **Sentadas** (left two figures) and **Sentadas I** (right), Susana Espinosa, 1979. *Slab construction, clay strips, engobes, oxide stain, glaze, 28″, 23″, 23″ (71.1, 58.4, 58.4 cm) from left to right. Courtesy of the artist. Photograph by Jochi Melero.*

Shaping space with slabs

This activity emphasizes repetition: repetition of positive and negative shapes and spaces. Encourage students to vary the sizes and orientation of these shapes and spaces.

Materials: Clay, work boards, sticks (optional), rolling pin, clay tool or pencil, slip.

Directions:
1. Wedge some clay, shape it into a ball, and flatten it. Roll or throw a clay slab. You might wish to leave the rough edges of the clay as they are, or cut the clay into a shape that you like. Your shape can be curved, geometric or free form.
2. Make two or three cuts into, but not all the way across, the slab.

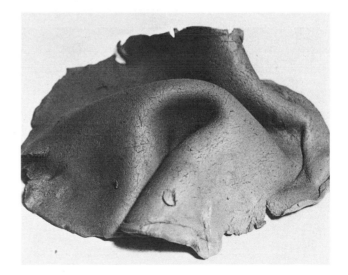

Let a slab gently fold and come to rest on its own.

Cutting into the slab.

3. Carefully lift, move, bend, fold or twist one of the sections to make it three-dimensional. Experiment with a few different arrangements.
4. Expand the negative and positive shapes and spaces that you have created. Repeat them in some way to unify your sculpture. You can cut shapes out of the slab.
5. Turn the sculpture as you work so that you can see it from many points of view. Try to involve your sculpture in space as much as possible.

Repeating negative and positive shapes.

Moving a shape to make it three-dimensional.

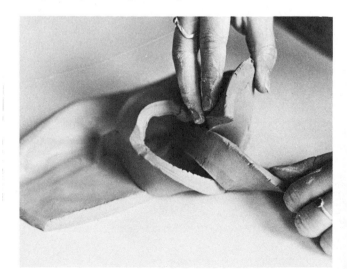

The sculpture continues.

6. Join shapes to one another by scoring.
7. Give your sculpture a title.
8. You are finished when:
    You have positive and negative shapes and spaces which repeat.
    The shapes and spaces within the sculpture vary in size and placement.
    All parts are sturdy and firmly attached.
    The surface of your sculpture complements and unifies the form.

Students rolled clay slabs, then cut and coded them according to numbered paper patterns. Fired and glazed pieces are reassembled into a large wall sculpture. **Ceramic Mural** by children grades 1–6. *Photograph by Jim Fry.*

Slab sculpture example, Anne Hinckley, grade 8.

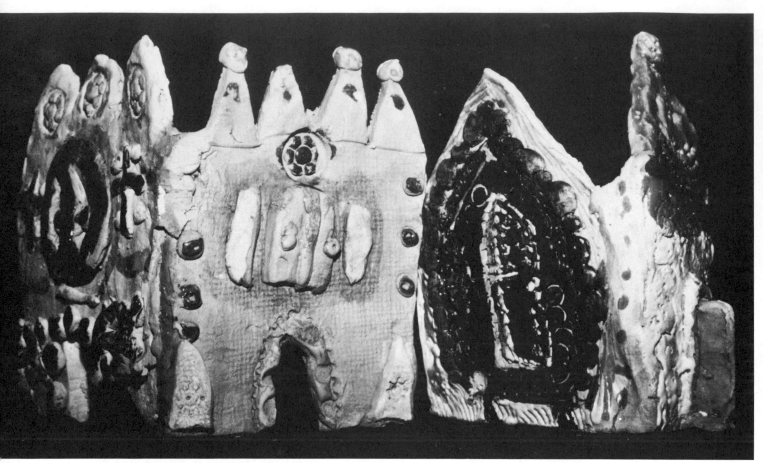

Clay relief architecture by 4th graders. Photograph by Valerie Kemp.

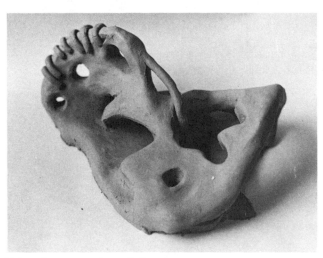

Slab sculpture example, grade 8.

Large slab sculptures

Slabs, shaped in a variety of different ways, can be combined to create large sculptures. Slab experiments also lend themselves to small group projects. After each individual shapes one slab form, the group must combine all the individual forms into one large sculpture. Due to the size and weight of the clay pieces and the degree of cooperation required, group experiments work best with older students.

Take a few minutes for practice of previously suggested techniques. Then students will need some time to explore the new possibilities on their own. Firing these experiments might prove difficult, due to their size. This is a good exploratory activity to use before asking individuals to create finished sculptures using the slab method.

House, Martha Rodriquez, age 17. *Slab construction.*

Clay slabs were cut, designed, textured and then joined to create these delightful buildings. The same activity can be given to students of varying ages and the results will be very different.

Summary of slab sculpture concepts

In clay slab sculpture, students again use concepts of **negative and positive shape, repetition** and **variety of form,** and **the relationship of space to mass.** Slab experiments require more clay, skill, concentration and care. To explore the slab method, students must be sensitive to the nature of clay. With these clay projects, students can learn the stretchiness of clay, its ability at the **leather hard** stage to retain a specific shape, and its tendency to shrink during drying. Rolling and throwing techniques, draping, folding and the use of an **armature** should become familiar to students who make clay slab sculpture.

Composition

The term **composition** refers to the way individual forms are arranged to create a whole. Sculptors arrive at arrangements by planning and by experimenting with the placement of forms.

When art principles are shown and discussed, students can recognize and understand on an intellectual and verbal level that which they see and feel intuitively. By basing lessons on one or more art principles, a teacher can give students something to look for and work with. At the same time students learn to identify, discuss and appreciate other works of art. Art principles provide students with ideas for organizing clay forms. Once they have done something experimentally, they can easily devise their own organizational patterns.

Directions, patterns of growth and progressions can be drawn with a few simple lines. Here are suggestions for drawing horizontal, vertical, diagonal, spiral, concentric, radiating, branching and progressing lines.

The artist Boccioni was leader of the Italian Futurist movement, a movement in which artists tried to show the dynamic "lines of force" characteristic of particular objects. Children can relate the "motions" suggested in this sculpture to the motions of a fist. **Boccioni's Fist — Lines of Force II,** *Giacomo Balla, 1915. Brass, 13½″ × 30″ × 10″ (80 × 76.2 × 25.4 cm). Courtesy Hirshhorn Museum and Sculpture Garden, Smithsonian Institution, Washington, D.C.*

Repetition of form

A sculpture that communicates a sense of unity or wholeness often is made of forms that are similar to each other in shape. The forms in a sculpture may be predominantly angular, curved, organic or geometric. To begin composing in clay, children can create several forms that are similar in shape yet varied in size. For example, in *Boccioni's Fist — Lines of Force II*, all the shapes are similar. All have curves of varying length and direction, sharp edges and sharp points.

Direction or motion

Often a sculpture can appear dynamic, or in motion. Sculptors create this illusion through the shape of each form and the direction or motion that the sculptor suggests. Horizontal sculptures seem static. Diagonal sculptures appear dynamic. Curvilinear sculptures seem more easygoing. Each of the sculptures pictured here illustrates a different direction and a different kind of implied motion.

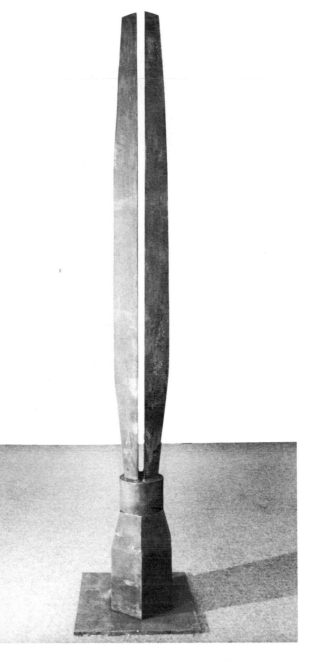

Unlike the forms in *Mauro Column* and *Avenger*, the coiled forms in this sculpture are delicate, capricious and flirtacious. They burst out in all directions from a center line, suggesting an ongoing, explosive energy. The pointed tips of the coiled forms seem to tickle and tantalize, just as do flames in a fire. The bright red-orange color of this sculpture dramatizes the overall effect. **Firedance,** Diane Kaiser, 1978. *Fired clay painted with acrylic, 9″ × 11″ × 3″ (22.9 × 27.9 × 7.62 cm). Collection of Mr. and Mrs. Erwin Marke, Brooklyn, New York. Photograph courtesy of the artist.*

In this sculpture positive and negative vertical forms direct the viewer's vision upward. Subtle curves contribute to the illusion of upward motion and counter the feeling that the two vertical forms might split apart and tumble down. Beverly Pepper creates large, freestanding sculptures in a variety of media. Her sculptures often show strong, conflicting directional thrusts. **Mauro Column,** Beverly Pepper, 1980. *Cast iron, 101¾″ × 11¼″ × 11¼″ (258 × 28.6 × 28.6 cm). Courtesy Andre Emmerich Gallery, New York. Photograph by Grant Barker.*

Ernst Barlach, a German Expressionist sculptor, often created works which express basic human emotions. The figure here has a horizontal/vertical stance, implying forward motion. The folds of the Avenger's robe do not flow gently around his body. Instead triangular shapes point straight forward, emphasizing the single-mindedness of a person determined to seek revenge. **Avenger (Der Racher),** Ernst Barlach, 1914. *Bronze, 17⅛″ × 23½″ × 9″ (43.5 × 59.7 × 22.8 cm). Courtesy Hirshhorn Museum and Sculpture Garden, Smithsonian Institution, Washington, D.C.*

Spiral, concentric and branching clay.

Patterns of growth

Forms within a sculpture may be arranged according to one of several growth patterns. A sculpture may seem to spiral much the way a snail grows its shell. A sculpture may be based on a concentric arrangement, the way a tree trunk develops new rings. Forms in a sculpture may be arranged in a branching pattern, like veins in a leaf, the branches of a tree or antlers of a deer. In some sculptures, individual forms radiate from a center point, like the legs of a spider, or the sun's rays.

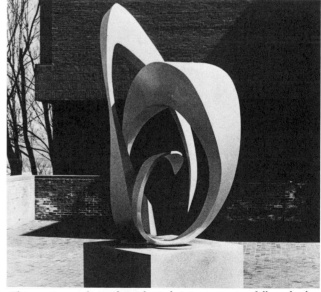

This continuous loop of metal spirals into space, gracefully and subtly changing directions. It contrasts dramatically with the solid, textured, closed form of the science center in the background. **Variations II,** Russell Jacques, 1978. *Metal, 168″ × 72″ × 72″ (427 × 183 × 183 cm). Merrill Science Center, Amherst College, Amherst, Massachusetts.*

This sculpture's concentric arrangement was inspired by children's games that Ms. Kaiser saw while touring Mexico. **Ready, Set**, Diane Kaiser, 1974. *Terra cotta, 30″ diameter, 2″ high (76.2 × 5.1 cm). Collection of the artist. Photograph courtesy of the artist.*

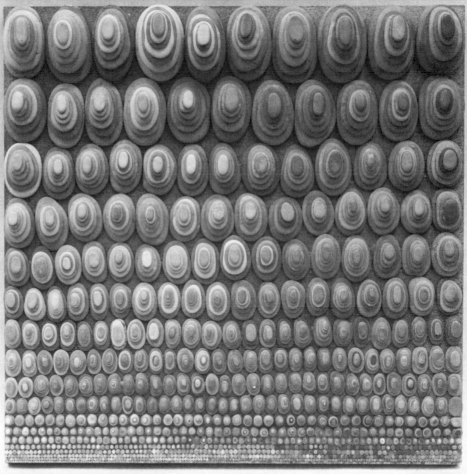

This sculpture was created from pebbles worn smooth and flat, and was assembled according to size. Each pile of rocks is a progression. The movement from the sculpture's bottom to top is a progression, too. **Eighteen Rows**, Mary Bauermeister, 1962–68. *17¾″ × 17¾″ (45 × 45 cm). Courtesy Smith College Museum of Art, Northampton, Masschusetts. Gift of Mrs. Holger Cahill.*

Progressions

Individual forms may be arranged on the basis of some kind of progression. Forms can progress from thick and bulky to light and airy. Small forms can lead to large forms. Static forms may progress to forms which appear to have motion. Rough forms can gradate to smooth ones. Closed forms can lead to open forms.

Following are two activities for exploring composition in clay sculpture.

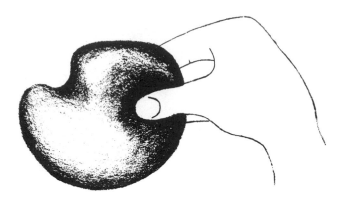

Poke in.

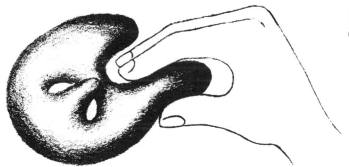

Pull out, always in the same direction.

Composition in the round

This exercise stresses similarity of form, variety of size and direction or motion. These are principles to consider while modeling a clay composition.

Directions:
1. Wedge clay, pat it into a ball, and poke one or two places that go in or through.
2. Think about various directions or motions, such as horizontal, vertical, diagonal, curving or radiating. Pull and model two or three protuberances that seem to reach out or to move in one direction.
3. Think about the kinds of forms you are creating. Are they curvy? Pointed? Angular? Keep the forms similar, but vary the sizes.
4. Think about the kind of movement that your sculpture exhibits. Is it fast, straight, rolling, spiralling, bouncy, etc.?
5. Give your sculpture a title.
6. Your sculpture is finished when:
   It is sturdy.
   It is smooth.
   It has direction.
   Its shapes are similar, but different in size.
   It is interesting from all points of view.

Shape your sculpture according to a direction or motion.

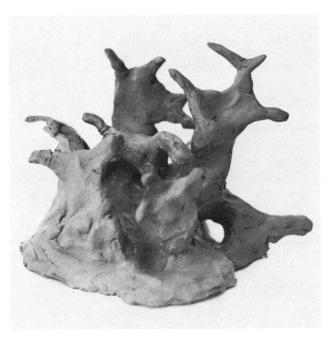

This sculpture is based on the form of a pinecone. The sculptures that come out of this activity often are reminiscent of forms from nature. Have shells, seed pods, rocks, branches and bones available for observation to make this activity more meaningful.

Branching Form, Josh Wolk, age 10.

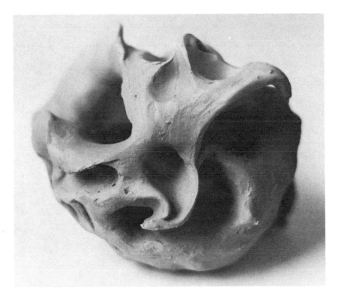

Folding, Wendy Walsh. *Collection of the artist.*

Sculptural Form, Lynne Goldman.

Composition in relief

In this activity clay forms are attached to a slab base, creating a sculpture in relief (see Chapter Four). The same activity could be done without a slab base, but it would be more difficult. Many clay parts must be joined together here, making this a more advanced activity than the preceding one.

Materials: Clay, work boards, slip, clay tools.

Directions:
1. Wedge clay and divide it into two balls. Roll or throw a slab from one ball.
2. Use the other ball to create five to seven forms that are similar in nature, but different in size. You may choose to make all coils, all pinch pots, all geometric shapes, all torn shapes, and so on.

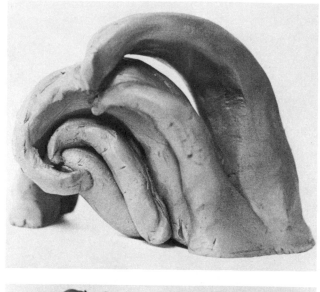

Arrangements based on direction, growth patterns, and progressions.

Forms that are similar in nature, but varied in size.

3. Arrange the clay forms on your slab according to some direction, motion, growth pattern, or progression. Try at least two different arrangements. Your forms may project into space.
4. When you find the arrangement that you like best, attach the forms to the slab. Smooth them.
5. Use fingers or a clay tool to shape the slab base. Accentuate your chosen direction, progression or growth pattern. Poke a hole about ½ inch or 1¼ centimeters from the top if you wish to use the slab as a plaque.

Summary of composition concepts

Though arranging forms according to an **organizing principle** may seem confining, the opposite is true. A **motion, direction, progression,** or **pattern of growth** presents students with a problem to solve. Once their sculpture begins to take shape, students find possibilities for creating variations. Students can learn to use **composition concepts** such as **vertical, horizontal, diagonal, spiral, concentric, branching** and **radiating**. Composition concepts can help students look at the world around them and see design.

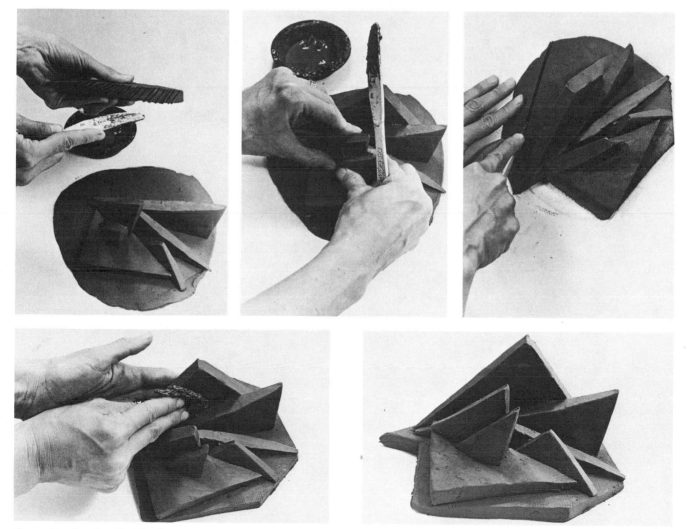

Composition based on the triangle.

Alternating finger textures make a pattern.

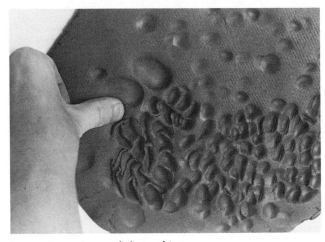

Separate impressions made by touching.

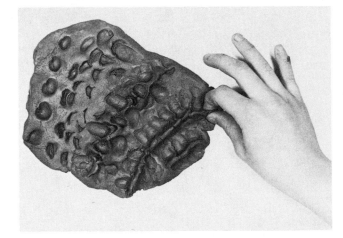

Pinching a texture.

Texture

The term **texture** is used to describe the quality of a surface — its roughness or smoothness. To create a texture, a large portion of a surface must be covered with repeated impressions. Texture can be created by rolling a clay slab onto a piece of cloth, such as burlap. An impression can be repeated many times to create a texture. Following are two exercises for practice in creating texture. The first exercise involves only hands and fingers. The second explores the potential of clay tools.

Textures made by pressing with a finger.

Texturing with fingers

Directions:
1. Roll, throw or pat a slab.
2. Use your fingers to create as many different kinds of textures as possible by pushing into the clay. Gently move your fingertips over each texture to feel differences and similarities.
   > Make some impressions close to one another but separate.
   > Make some impressions that connect.
   > Change the pressure that you use, to make shallow and deep impressions.
   > Pull your fingers through the clay.
   > Pinch a texture.
3. Turn your clay over. Make a pattern with your impressions.
   > Repeat one kind of impression over and over again.
   > Change the direction or the interval of your fingertips, and continue making impressions.
4. Roll tiny balls or coils and press them onto your clay to create a texture.
5. What do your textures look like or suggest? Rocks, bricks, water, hair, tiles, fish scales, leaves?

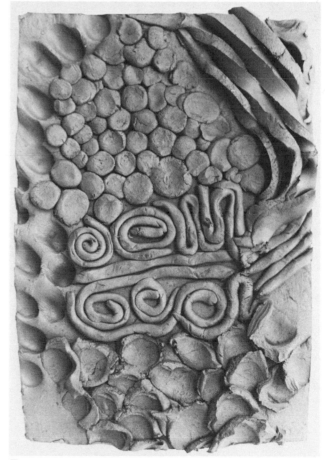

Textures made by pressing small pieces of clay onto a slab.

This three-dimensional chart is posted in the art room where children can touch it, place their fingers in the grooves and guess how each texture was made. These tiles were made by six-year-old children, fired, coated with clear polymer medium and glued to a Masonite base. **Finger texture display.**

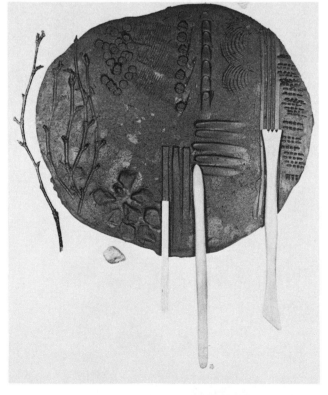

Clay tools. Any object that makes an impression in clay may be used as a clay tool. Shells, buttons, keys, forks, pencils, pastry tools, twigs and leaves all may be used as clay tools. It can be helpful to have a few tools that are made especially for clay.

Texturing with tools

Directions:
1. Roll, throw or pat a slab.
2. Choose one clay tool. Press it into the clay many times in one section of your slab. You have created a textured area.
3. Use the same tool in a different way to create a second textured area. You might hold the tool at a new angle, use the other end, press harder, drag it, poke with it, or press the whole tool flat into the clay.

4. Continue using different parts of the same tool until you have created at least five different textured areas.
5. Look closely at each of your textured areas. Figure out what each texture might represent (snow, freckles, rocks, grass, balloons, etc.).

6. Choose a second tool and repeat the whole process. See how many different textures you can make from one tool.
7. Move your fingertips gently over the textures you have just made. Can you feel the differences?

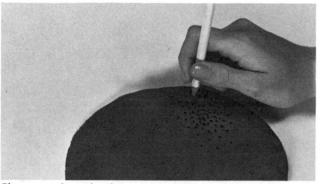

Choose one clay tool and press it into the clay many times to make a textured area.

Second textured area made by the side of the same tool.

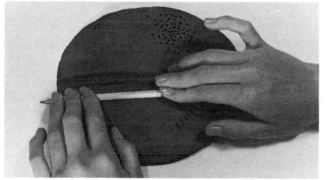

Third textured area made by the other end of the same tool.

An array of textures made by one tool.

Try a second tool.

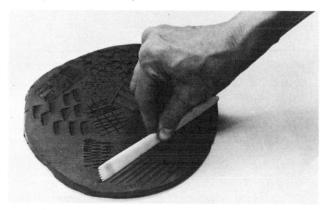

Make at least five textured areas with that tool.

After experimenting with finger textures and clay tool textures and after studying fish, students produced these plaques. Students were told to include all parts of the fish — rear fin, belly fin, middle fins, gas bladder, gills and eyes — in their clay models. **Fish Plaques** by students, age 6.

Guidelines for use of texture

Texture can add to or detract from a sculptural form. When everything is textured or when textures are randomly pressed into the clay, the sculpture will appear to be a jumble of confusing impressions. Textures will have more impact if they are chosen wisely. Give students a few guidelines. This helps them to be more thoughtful and selective in applying texture.

☐ Textures can be used to imitate textures seen elsewhere, such as hair, fish scales, basket weave, and corduroy.

☐ In a nonobjective sculpture, choose textures that complement the direction or motion of the sculptural form. Notice how the diagonal forms are exaggerated by the texture in *Column of Peace* by Antoine Pevsner.

☐ Texture can be used dramatically to accent one area, while the rest of the sculpture may remain smooth.

☐ By repeating a texture in more than one area, as in *Habitat* by Mirtala Bentov, the sculptor can give unity to a sculpture. A repeated texture can lead a viewer's eye through the clay composition.

When many textures are used in a sculpture, some should contrast, or stand out from, one another. A sculptor can achieve this by putting smooth areas next to textured ones and by varying the direction or depth of a texture. Some textures might be created by using lines, others by using shapes or dots.

Be sure that your texture extends to all parts of a shape so that the whole area stands out and is unified as a shape.

When working in relief, consider adding texture to the raised forms, leaving the background smooth; or you can give texture to the background, leaving the raised forms smooth. Either technique will help make the forms easy to recognize.

Not all of these guidelines will apply to every sculpture project. Choose the suggestions that make most sense in the activities that you are doing. Add some other guidelines.

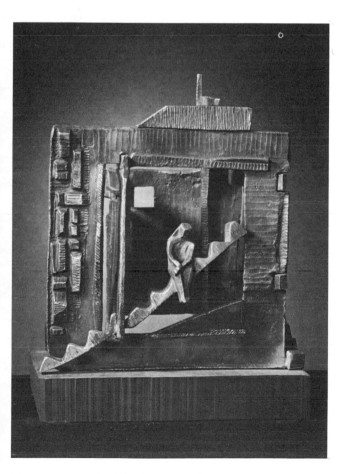

The textures in each of the slab sections of *Habitat* were treated with linear textures suggestive of building materials. Notice how the sculptor achieved contrast within this sculpture. **Habitat,** Mirtala Bentov. *Bronze. Courtesy Pucker/Safrai Gallery, Boston, Massachusetts.*

The textured surfaces of each form follow the shape of the piece and accentuate directions at the same time. **Column of Peace,** Antoine Pevsner, 1954. *Bronze, 52" × 33" × 17¼" (132.1 × 83.8 × 43.8 cm). Courtesy Hirshhorn Museum and Sculpture Garden, Smithsonian Institution, Washington, D.C.*

Summary of texture concepts

Surface patterns may be **connected, separate, deep, shallow** or **repetitive,** with **smooth spaces** interspersed in a number of ways. Students can learn the varied effects of texture while they use concepts of **contrast, rhythm, direction** and **balance** in their artwork and discussion.

Though there are many different textures used in this work, the images are still clear. How did the artist achieve clarity and make the monster stand out from the house and the background? **Monster Plaque,** Janice Szymaszek.

4

SCULPTING
IN RELIEF

This contemporary relief sculpture moves from low to high relief. The rough-textured beard and the pages of the book stand out from the otherwise smooth surfaces of the sculpture. **Scholar,** David Aronson, 1978. *Clay model, 9″ × 5¾″ × 1½″ (23 × 15 × 4 cm). Courtesy Pucker/Safrai Gallery, Boston, Massachusetts. Photograph by Barney Burstein.*

Al sculptures can be divided into two categories — freestanding or relief. **Freestanding** sculpture is not attached to a background slab. Freestanding sculpture will be explored in later chapters.

Relief sculptures are forms associated with a background surface. The sculpture extends from, or is recessed into, the background. The viewer cannot see all the sides of the sculpture. The height of the sculpture from the background and the depth of the sculpture are described by such terms as intaglio, sunk, low (or *bas*, pronounced "bah") and high.

Relief sculptures often show scenes from the everyday life of a tribe or culture. Each panel of this door depicts Nigerian children playing a different game. Notice the variety of designs and textures carved into the children's clothing and into the borders. **Carved Door,** Lamidi Fakeyi, 1977. *Mahogany, 75¼" × 29⅝" (193 × 76 cm). Collection of Reverend Frances Potter Gamble. Photograph courtesy Mead Art Museum, Amherst College, Amherst, Massachusetts.*

An **intaglio relief** has lines etched into a flat surface. **Sunk relief** involves larger areas, often faces and figures, pressed or sunk below the flat surface. In a **low relief** sculpture, the forms project a little bit above the surface. Forms in a **high relief** sculpture are partly or wholly freed from the flat background.

Like painting or drawing, the relief method lends itself to picture making, with an important difference. Relief sculptures are three-dimensional. Carved, incised and modeled from durable materials, some relief sculptures have survived for thousands of years, providing one of the main pictorial sources of information about life in ancient times.

Stamp seals and cylindrical seals were used thousands of years ago in the Middle East. They were pressed into pieces of clay to seal packages, to identify them and to prevent thievery during delivery. The seals are cut, or hollowed out, in intaglio form. When pressed into clay, the resulting forms appear in relief. **Cylindrical Stone Seal.** *Collection of the author.*

In ancient times Assyrian palaces were covered with alabaster carved in low relief and brilliantly painted. Here the eagle-headed deity performs a fertilization ceremony. Notice the simple, very effective line designs on the wings, clothing and plants. The sculptor made the designs stand out visually by placing them next to very smooth surfaces. **Winged, Eagle-Headed Figure,** *Assyrian, 9th century* B.C. *From the ruins of Nimrod. Gift of Reverend Henry Lobdell, M.D. Courtesy Mead Art Museum, Amherst College.*

Reliefs that decorate a civilization's government buildings, palaces and houses of worship usually depict legends, myths, ceremonies and historical events important to the people's culture. Relief sculptures often commemorate heroes or illustrate episodes in the lives of such religious figures as Christ and Buddha. Like early paintings and drawings, the forms pictured in relief usually carry some symbolic or special meaning.

Reliefs frequently appear on weapons, ritual objects and personal artifacts. These intricate relief sculptures identify, ornament and glorify items important to an individual's honor or survival. Coins are an interesting example of relief sculpture.

The relief method is an excellent way to create a picture in clay. Instead of drawing on a two-dimensional surface, each part of a composition can be modeled. Complex pictures can be made using this method because support of carved pieces is not a problem.

A lesson on relief sculpture might follow themes from relief sculptures of the past. Students can model self-portraits, scenes from daily life, historic events or an episode from a story. Commemorative medallions or coins, symbols for family seals and decorative tiles all are challenging and exciting projects.

In relief sculpture, students may have problems attaching clay forms securely onto the slab base and using texture to create a clear and "readable" image. It might help to review the sections on adding clay and on texture in Chapter Three.

Following are three different approaches to working in relief. Each requires different abilities and different skills, concepts and techniques.

Adding to a slab

Even young children can be successful using this relief method. Be sure the clay is very moist so that scoring is not necessary.

Materials: Moist clay, work boards, rolling pins, sticks (optional), clay tools.

Directions:
1. Wedge clay and roll out a slab. Be certain that it does not stick to your work surface.
2. Plan your form in terms of shape. Think of the parts (such as arms, legs and head) as simple basic shapes, forgetting details. It is helpful to draw a sketch before working in clay.

Think about the object or form in terms of basic shapes.

Form the shapes.

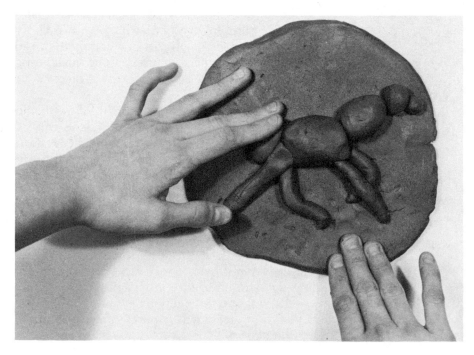

Pressing horse shapes onto a clay slab.

3. Use more clay to form the shapes you need. You may choose to roll balls and coils, or may model the shapes.
4. Press the clay forms onto your slab.

5. Join the clay forms by pushing, smoothing, and working with your fingers and thumbs. Move the clay as you work, raising and lowering different sections of your sculpture.

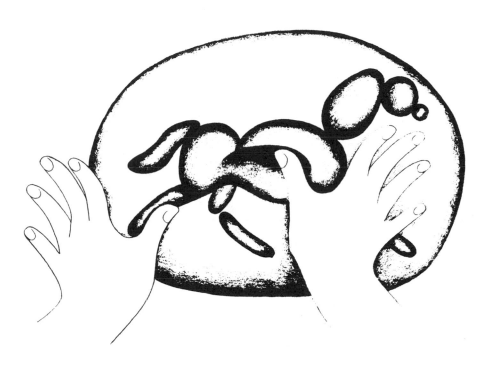

Join your shapes by pushing and smoothing.

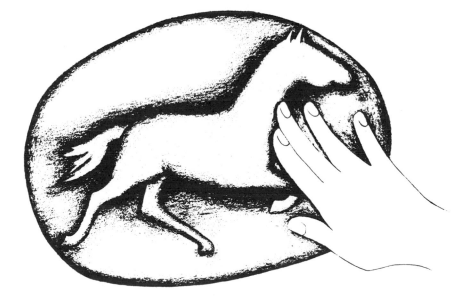

Smooth and clarify the edges of your clay form.

Add details and textures.

Four-, five-, and six-year-old children can form letters, people, animals, trees and designs from balls and coils of many lengths and sizes. They can learn to press and smooth clay pieces onto a clay slab. Children enjoy adding features and tiny details with a pencil or clay tool. **Self Portrait,** by student, age 4½.

6. Go around the edge of the entire form with your fingers or a clay tool. Be sure that all parts are firmly attached to the slab base.
7. Use clay tools to add texture and details. For contrast and clarity you may give texture to the main form and leave the background smooth, or give texture to the background and leave the main form smooth.

8. If you wish the relief to be used as a wall plaque poke a hole about ½ inch or 1¼ centimeters from the top of the sculpture. Because clay shrinks as it dries, make the hole big enough to allow for shrinkage.

9. You are finished when:
   All forms are well attached.
   You have used texture to make your main form stand out clearly from the background.

Seven- to nine-year-olds can create more complex compositions, with more than one figure or object, big and little forms, etc. They can be much more selective about the way they use texture for contrast between foreground and background. **My House,** by Josh, age 7.

Older students can create detailed compositions using a variety of techniques — incising, pulling, pushing, carving and texturing with clay tools and adding forms by scoring. **Me in My Halloween Costume (The Hunchback of Notre Dame),** by Rachel Topal, age 10.

Lightly draw the main large shapes.

Modeling a slab

This method is more difficult than the first method because it requires more planning and hand control. Students should strive to make figures distinct. They should also try to use more than one level of relief.

Materials: Clay, work boards, rolling pin, sticks (optional), clay tools.

Directions:
1. Wedge clay and roll a thick slab (about ¾ inch or 2 centimeters thick). Be certain that your slab does not stick to your work surface.
2. Using a pencil or clay tool, *lightly* draw on your slab the main shapes of the picture you are making. If you press too hard, you will cut the clay into pieces. If this happens, start over.

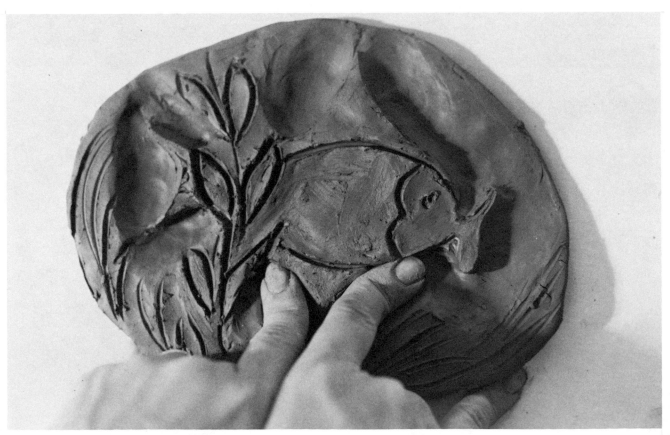

Push clay away from the main forms using fingers.

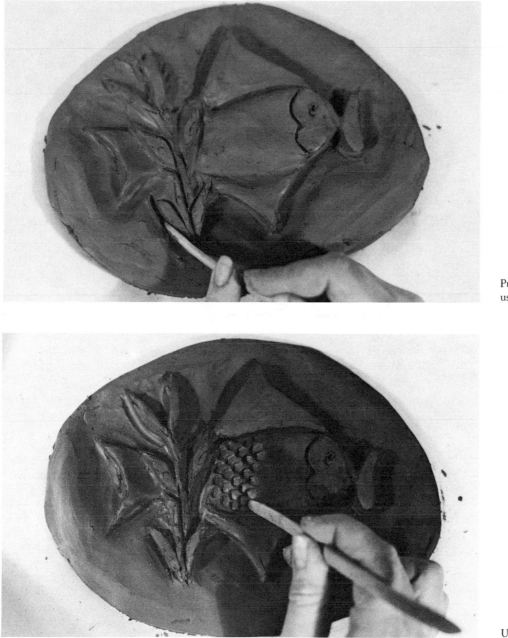

Push clay away from the main form using clay tools.

Use clay tools to add texture.

3. Raise the main form so that it is in low relief. Use fingers, thumbs, and clay tools to push clay from the background and sides into the main form to make it rise. Push clay away from the edges of the main form to make it distinct.

4. Use clay tools to add texture and detail. One finger can act as a support while the other delicately models the clay. Do not make clay forms too thin. Thin forms crack easily when they dry.

Use fingers to smooth and clarify forms.

Finished fish plaque by Kay Lerner.

Raising a main form by pushing clay.

5. Smooth where desired. Poke a hole ½ inch or 1¼ centimeters from the top of the sculpture if you wish to use your relief sculpture as a wall plaque.
6. You are finished when:
    The forms and figures in your relief are distinct.
    You have at least two levels of relief.
    Textures extend to the edges of each area or shape.
    You have achieved contrast between textured areas.
    The edges are smooth and the piece stands as a complete unit.

Shaping three-dimensional details. One finger can act as a support while the other delicately models clay. Be careful not to make clay forms too thin. Thin forms crack easily.

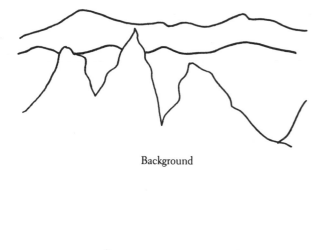

Background

Middle ground

Perspective

This relief method combines the various levels of relief (intaglio, sunk, low, and high) with basic concepts of perspective. Students are asked to draw on paper a simple scene with a clear foreground, middle ground and background. To do this they may need to review a few basic notions about perspective.

In general, when looking at a scene the *distant or background objects* (mountains, trees, sky) seem to be highest in the picture plane, small, indistinct and close together. *Middle ground objects* are midway between the background and foreground, often in the middle of the picture plane. *Close-up or foreground objects* generally are low in the picture plane and bigger and clearer than background objects. Foreground objects may be more distant from one another, rounded or more three-dimensional and may overlap the middle and background objects.

Before beginning to work in clay, students should form a plan of action. They need to decide what forms to sink into the background, where to push excess clay, what forms to raise and which forms to have stand out dramatically in high relief. This is challenging but not hard to do. Simple drawings on paper work best. These take on a totally different appearance when modeled in three dimensions. Details can be added later.

Foreground

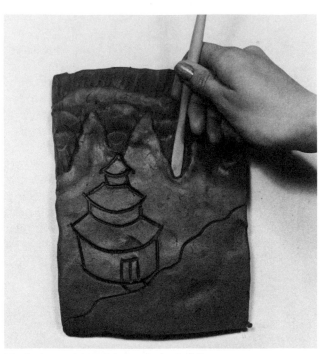

The background is sunk below the level of the mountains.

Extra clay is added to make the middle ground pavilion more three-dimensional.

Materials: Clay, work boards, rolling pin, sticks (optional), clay tools, slip.

Directions:
1. Wedge clay and roll a thick slab (about ¾ inch or 2 centimeters thick). Be certain that it does not stick to your work surface.
2. Working from your paper drawing, lightly sketch the main forms from the background, middle ground and foreground onto your slab. Use fingers and clay tools to raise and lower the forms so that you have three levels of relief.

Details are added before scoring the foreground figure.

Adding the foreground figure by scoring.

3. Model each relief level with fingers and clay tools, adding appropriate textures and details. Remember that background textures and details are smaller, higher, and less distinct than foreground ones. Sink some areas below the surface. Etch some details in intaglio relief.
4. Add on at least one form by scoring. Make it stand out dramatically in high relief as your center of interest.
5. You are finished when:
       All forms are well attached.
       Figures and forms are distinct.
       There are at least three levels of relief.
       One form stands out dramatically in high relief.
       Textured areas contrast with one another.
       The edges are smooth and the piece stands as a complete unit.

Finished relief sculpture by Simone Topal, age 15.

Summary of relief sculpture concepts

Relief sculptures may have images raised or recessed to various levels such as **intaglio, sunk, low** (or **bas**) and **high** relief. Children can learn to add clay, model and use perspective (**background, middle ground, foreground**) in clay slab relief sculptures. Students should understand the difference between relief and freestanding sculptures, and should learn to see basic shapes in forms. They should learn to plan a center of interest in their relief designs.

5
ANIMALS

The unusual yet characteristic position of *Faun* communicates a sense of the animal while it helps make the animal sturdy. **Faun,** John Flannagan, *circa 1930. Bronze with cast stone base, 14½" (35.6 cm). Courtesy Smith College Museum of Art, Northampton, Massachusetts. Gift of Mr. Emil Arnold.*

There are many ways to sculpt animals. Small animals may be modeled by pulling appendages from a thick clay mass. Animals that are close to the ground, such as turtles and alligators, or in a resting position may be made by draping a thick clay slab over an armature. Larger animals may be sculpted from thick balls and coils that are modeled separately and then joined together. The techniques may be combined and a clay animal project can have added texture and design. There are many possibilities.

Before working with clay, sculptors should be well acquainted with the subtle characteristics of their animals. Pictures, movies and dramatizations of animals help pinpoint the actions and features that make each animal unique. Encourage students to think about how an animal moves, where it lives, what it eats, how it raises its young, how it protects itself from other animals, as well as its shape, proportions, textures and coloring. In an animal sculpture, it is details such as a tilted head, a twitching ear or tail, or the way an animal scratches or sits that catch the viewer's attention and communicate something about the nature of that animal.

Sometimes students begin sculpting with one animal in mind, only to find that their sculpture turns out looking like another kind of animal. Discuss this possibility beforehand to make it less disturbing. Should it happen, students should go with the animal that is evolving from the clay. Sometimes parts of an animal sculpture may droop or collapse. Such events may be looked upon as messages from the clay, suggesting that the sculptor change the position or stance of an animal to fit the collapse. Sometimes this makes the animal more interesting.

The following activities describe procedures for modeling freestanding animals. Freestanding sculptures support themselves and are not attached to a background. It is more difficult than it appears to make a four-legged animal support itself. Let students try the first two techniques by making a quick animal. Allow about five minutes for children to complete the first animal. Discuss problems. Then demonstrate the second technique. Allow about five minutes for students to complete the second animal. Then compare results. These quick sculptures are referred to as **clay sketches.** Clay sketches are a good way to gain experience quickly. Slab animals are for the more advanced student.

Animals will stand better if the legs are thick and the body is thin. A thick clay slab base or a new position can help, too. Small terra-cotta figures such as this one were popular offerings at all kinds of sanctuaries during the Greek Dark Ages. **Horse and Rider,** *Greek, Attic? 6th century* B.C.*? Terra cotta, 5¾" × 5½" (15 × 14 cm). Courtesy Mead Art Museum, Amherst College, Amherst, Massachusetts. Gift of Paul D. Morgan.*

By adding animal appendages to pots or hollow forms, a sculptor can create a functional sculpture. **Seated Dog Vessel,** *artist unknown, Colima, Mexico, 700–1000* A.D. *Burnished tan clay with traces of black paint. Courtesy Mount Holyoke College Art Museum, South Hadley, Massachusetts. Gift of Mr. and Mrs. James F. Mathias.*

Modeling small animals

Materials: Moist clay, work boards, clay tools.

Directions: Do not have a specific animal in mind.

1. Wedge a ball of clay about the size of a lemon. Small balls are easier for young children to handle. Roll the ball into a thick oval shape.
2. Model the head and neck by squeezing gently with your thumb and first finger a little way in from the end. Don't squeeze too hard!
3. Draw a cross on the rest of the oval. You can do this with your finger or a clay tool.
4. Model the legs by pulling the clay gently from each section of the cross. Keep the legs thick and sturdy. Vary the length of the legs and the thickness of the body to change the animal's shape.

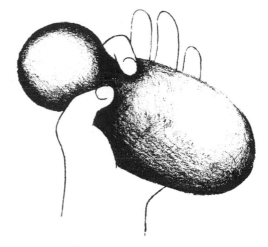

Roll a flat sausage and squeeze a neck.

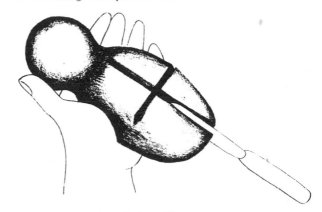

Mark a large cross where the legs will go.

The beast's position on his back alleviates the problem of support. The artist was free to form decorative and fanciful appendages. Texture has been used selectively and dramatically. Where has the artist used coiled forms? **Mythical Beast,** *artist unknown, Japan. Bronze, 6¼″ × 8½″ (16 × 22 cm). Courtesy George Walter Vincent Smith Art Museum, Springfield, Massachusetts.*

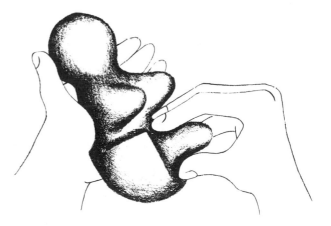

Pull a thick leg from each square. Let the shape of the body suggest an animal to you.

5. Model, as needed, the features of the head, ears, nose, jaws, horns, hooves or toes.
6. Position your animal. What is your animal doing? Is it standing, sitting, scratching, running, pointing, sleeping?
7. Smooth your animal and reinforce any weak parts. Add appropriate textures. Be selective! Follow the form of the animal when adding texture.

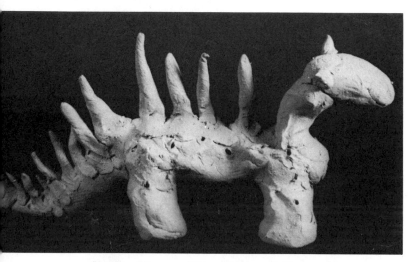

Imaginary Dinosaur, Allison Grant, age 7. Photograph by Valerie Kemp.

Position your animal and add details.

Each animal here suggests its own decorative possibilities. What techniques were used to create the textures in *Poodle* and *Zebra*? Notice that the texture lines follow the shape of the animal. **Poodle** and **Zebra,** Jesus and Javier Carvajales. *Clay. Collection of the author.*

Although the legs and tails of these rabbits are missing, the viewer immediately recognizes their "rabbitness." To extend a project on animal sculpture, ask students to sculpt a baby animal or person to accompany the larger sculpture. Second sculptures usually are easier and faster to complete because students already have been through the process. **Mother and Baby Rabbit,** student, age 8.

Larger animals

Materials: Moist clay, work boards, slip, clay tools, newspaper.

Directions: Have an animal in mind before you begin.

1. Wedge a ball of clay and divide it into as many pieces as you need to make body parts. Shape each part — legs, body, head — by rolling and modeling.

2. Join pieces together by scoring.
3. Reinforce and smooth all joints.
4. Position your animal. Newspaper can be used to support heavy parts until they arc leather hard. Refine and smooth the entire animal.
5. Add appropriate textures and details.
6. Hollow out the thick parts when the sculpture is almost leather hard. If a sculpture is more than 1½ inches or 3.8 centimeters thick, it should be hollowed out. Don't make the clay too thin, though.

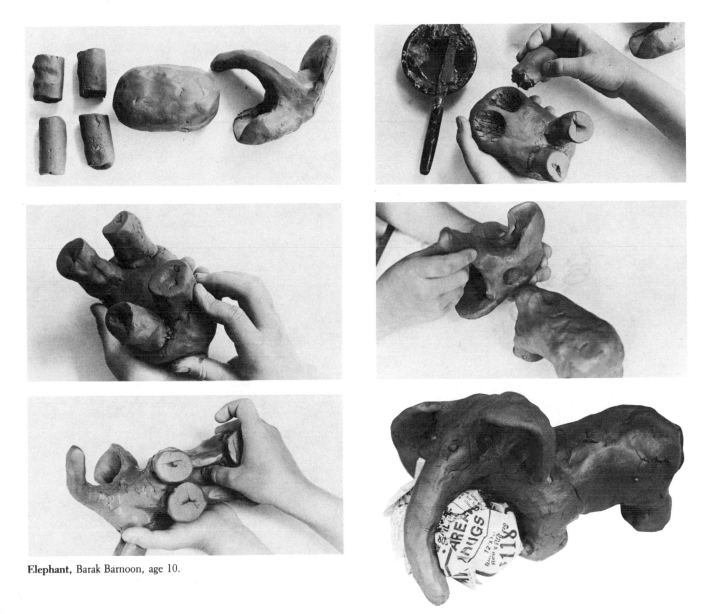

Elephant, Barak Barnoon, age 10.

This large animal sculpture was made by draping a clay slab over a plastic bag filled with vermiculite. Sand makes a good support, too. As the sculpture hardened, the plastic bag was opened, emptied and gently pulled out. Details and features were modeled and added on by scoring. **Penguin,** Julie Cain, age 13.

Animals by slab

Materials: Moist clay, work boards, rolling pin and sticks (optional), clay tools, newspaper, slip.

Directions:

1. Wedge a large ball of clay and roll or throw a thick slab.
2. Crush newspaper and shape it to form the main body of your animal. Tape newspaper together if necessary. Cardboard shapes may be used as an armature to support the weight of your clay animal until it is leather hard. Drape the clay slab over the armature. Raise additional parts such as legs, tails, paws and heads, using extra crushed newspaper.
3. Shape the clay slab around the armature.
4. Cut off the extra clay and keep it moist.
5. Use extra clay to reinforce weak areas and to add parts.
6. Smooth the entire sculpture. Add appropriate texture and detail.
7. Gently remove the newspaper when the sculpture is almost leather hard. Newspaper may be burned out in the kiln, if you plan to fire the piece, but tape would cause a terrible odor.

Alligator, Rachel Topal, age 5.

Turtle, Josh Wolk, age 10.

Animal groups

A larger and more complex sculpture can be made by grouping and connecting individual animals. A sculpture class could make animals from a chosen habitat and then use appropriate materials, such as rocks, sand, twigs and greens, to make a display. Zoo animals and circus scenes are popular themes for group sculptures.

Summary of animal sculpture concepts

When students sculpt animals, they learn how to model **protruding parts** and make a sculpture sturdy. Students can combine animal forms with the use of **texture,** and learn new ways to balance **positive and negative shapes** in their sculpture. Practice in modeling an animal's posture can lead students to observe more carefully the **postures** and **gestures** in the world around them.

Some parts of this beautifully-crafted sculpture were made by pressing clay slabs into plaster molds. When the shapes reached the leather hard stage, they were assembled and scored together. Other shapes, such as the animals and details, were made by modeling. **Noah's Ark,** Raul Dela Cerda, age 17.

6

Heads and Faces

Expression can be created with simplified forms, as seen in this serene African sculpture. **Top of Ceremonial Axe,** *Zaire, 18th century. Wood and metal, 15¾" (40 cm). Courtesy Smith College Museum of Art, Northampton, Massachusetts.*

Heads and faces provide rich subject matter and a good structure for exploring sculptural concepts. The design of the head incorporates numerous functions such as seeing, hearing, smelling, tasting, chewing, thinking and expressing emotions. The outer, visible part of the head takes its shape from the skull, an inner support structure. In addition, the many features of the face are arranged symmetrically, providing a format for the exploration of texture and design.

In sculpting a face or head, the sculptor shapes a character and a personality from a clay mass. Intentionally or not, as each feature is pulled, poked, or added, the personality of the head or face becomes further defined. Faces can turn out to be funny or scary, or may suggest a character type. Children can sculpt a head by developing the character that seems to emerge as they shape the clay.

As in all sculpting, sculptors must know their subjects. By feeling and studying how the skull supports and shapes their own heads and features, students come to know their subject through their sense of touch. They can apply this knowledge directly as they begin to model clay.

Ask students to close their eyes and place their fingertips at the back of their necks. Have them move their hands slowly up, past the hairline, the large bulge at the back of the skull, over the scalp, the forehead, eyebrows and eye sockets, and down to the bridge of the nose. Comment on each feature and its function. Point out the way each feature is shaped by the underlying skull and note the relationships between the features.

Where does this head follow the form of the skull? Where has the artist elaborated on the form? **Head of a Death God,** *Mexican, 900–1200 A.D. Stone, 7¾" × 3" × 2½" (19.6 × 7.6 × 6.4 cm). Courtesy Smith College Museum of Art, Northampton, Massachusetts.*

Contrast the head and face on *Ceremonial Axe* with the head and face of *Nimba Mask.* These heads come from tribes in different parts of Africa. In making each head, the artists used facial features, scarification patterns, hairstyles and headdresses to create a highly designed head. **Top of Ceremonial Axe,** *Zaire, 18th century. Wood and metal, 15¾" (40 cm). Courtesy Smith College Museum of Art, Northampton, Massachusetts.*

Each feature in this mask has been distorted, exaggerated or geometrized in some way. Notice the design techniques used in this striking mask. **Nimba Mask,** *the Baga Tribe, Guinea, West Africa. Wood, 35" (88.9 cm). Courtesy Pucker/Safrai Gallery, Boston, Massachusetts.*

Have the children feel the shapes of their ears. Point out that the hinge for the jawbone begins almost at the ears, and the jawbone gives shape to the chin and lips.

It is important to work toward exaggeration of facial features. The natural tendency is to be hesitant in shaping features, especially as a semblance of a face appears. Have children poke deeply into the clay, pull way out and try something a little crazy. It is easy to tone it down later.

Masks and heads from many cultures can show the varied ways in which heads and features have been interpreted. In three dimensions or in pictures, these also serve as a resource for design and texture ideas.

Clay Face, Nickie Smith, grade 2. Photograph by Valerie Kemp.

Clay Mask, Chris Rohan, grade 9.

Students can name the facial features that go in and those that come out. Make a list of features for future reference.

Faces in relief

This lesson can be used with children ages five and up. Because of its tactility, it also works well with a variety of special needs children.

There are several ways to approach sculpting a face in relief. Young children will benefit most by exploring and identifying the various facial features. Older children may focus on expression or emotion in a face. Exaggeration of features, as in a cartoon or caricature, is fun for all ages. To create a mask for a special occasion or to depict a character, your students can exaggerate features and add texture to the planes and features of the face.

Materials: Moist clay, clay tools.

Directions:

1. Wedge a large ball of clay and make a very thick slab. If you are making a mask, drape the slab over a domed newspaper armature to make it rounded.
2. Pull and model all of the features that protrude (or come out), such as eyebrows, nose, cheeks, chin and lips.
3. Poke all of the features that go in, such as eye sockets, nostrils and mouth. Poke some places all the way through if you wish.
4. Add on some features, such as ears, bushy eyebrows, a mustache or a large nose. Be sure that features are well attached.
5. Smooth and refine the whole sculpture.
6. Use a pointed stick or clay tool to add details and textures to hair, eyebrows, beards and mustaches.

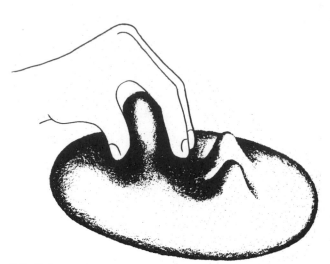

Pull all the protuberances.

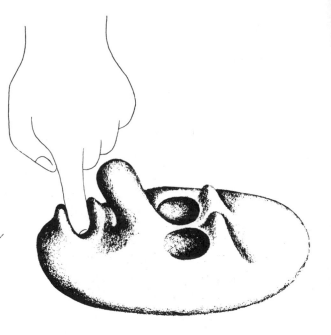

Poke all the indentations.

Add on extra clay.

Add details.

Heads in the round

The skills, concepts and techniques involved in creating a head in the round are complex. For this reason the following lesson probably would be best handled by students at least 12 years old.

A finished head must be hollow if it is to be fired in the kiln. A solid head would be very heavy and would most likely explode in the kiln because gases would build up in the clay. If this happened, other pieces in the kiln would be destroyed as well. At the same time, a clay head must be sturdy enough to withstand the pressure of poking, pulling and modeling without collapsing. If you plan to fire the pieces, be sure to wedge the clay before sculpting. (See Chapter One for instructions on wedging.)

There are two ways to solve this dilemma. The finished head can be hollowed out by cutting off the back, scooping out the clay and rejoining the pieces by scoring. Hair and other fine details can be added to the hollowed form.

Alternatively, an **armature** or inside support structure can be created for the head. Use of an armature means that much less clay will be required. By changing the size of the armature, the size of the sculpture may be changed. The armature can be extended to include the chest and arms if these are to be sculpted.

It is preferable to use an armature that does not have to be removed by cutting into the head. Newspaper is terrific for this. It is accessible, light and can be burned out in the kiln.

Following is a procedure for making a grapefruit-size head. A thick clay slab is draped over a newspaper armature and shaped. There is ample clay on the slab to shape all the parts of the face without adding any clay, except for the eyes, possibly the nose and the hair. The trick, as in all sculpting, is to have the clay moist but not sticky. If the clay is too dry it will crack, and problems will occur.

Materials: Newspaper, string, moist clay, work boards, clay tools, rolling pin, sticks (optional).

Clay Head, Dan Cronin, grade 8.

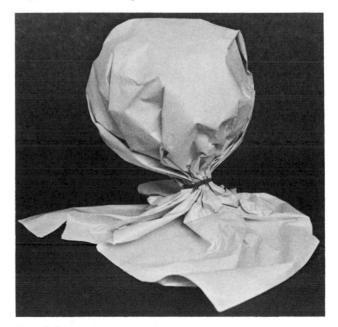

Crumpled paper armature.

Directions:
Step One: **Make a newspaper armature.**
1. Crumple a sheet of newspaper into a ball.
2. Place the newspaper ball inside a smooth piece of newspaper. Model the paper around the newspaper ball and fasten it with a string or a wire twist. Splay the gathered ends of the paper so they act as a base to hold the armature erect.

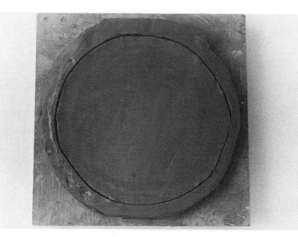

Clay slab circle.

Remove wedges.

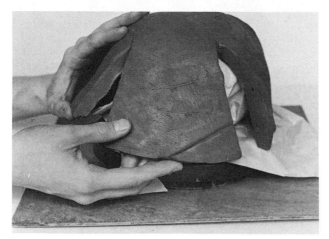

Work the four sections together.

Step Two: **Roll a thick clay slab and shape it over the armature.**

1. Roll a thick clay slab (about ¾ inch or 2 centimeters). Trace a circle with a diameter of about 9 inches or 23 centimeters, and cut it out of the slab.
2. Cut four wedges from the circle and remove them. Cover excess clay with plastic to keep it moist for later use.
3. Drape the clay slab over the newspaper armature, centering it.
4. Gently press the four sections together to close the "seams" as you turn the whole armature every few seconds. Let the head take shape naturally. Go with the shape that emerges as you press and turn, forming the neck.
5. Remove the wire twist from the base of the armature. Push the excess newspaper ends into the inside of the neck for additional support.

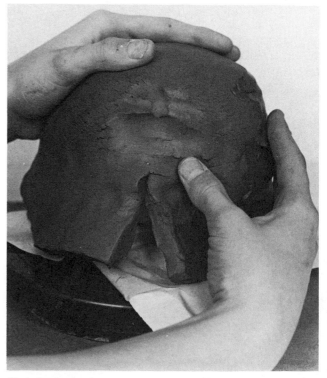

Close the clay head.

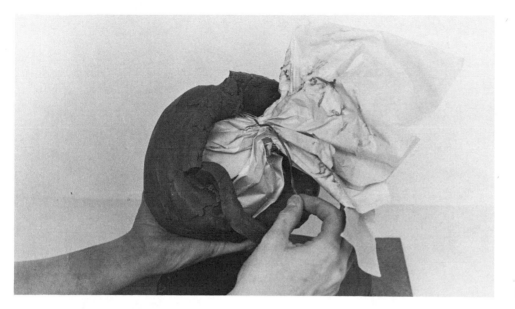

Remove wire twist.

Shape the neck.

Step Three: Shape the head.

1. Look at the shapes of your fellow students' heads. Use them as references while modeling your clay head.
2. Look closely at your clay head. Does it seem to have a front already? If not, decide where the face will be. Form the chin, the bulge at the back of the head, the forehead and the brows by pushing, pulling and modeling.

Form chin and back of head.

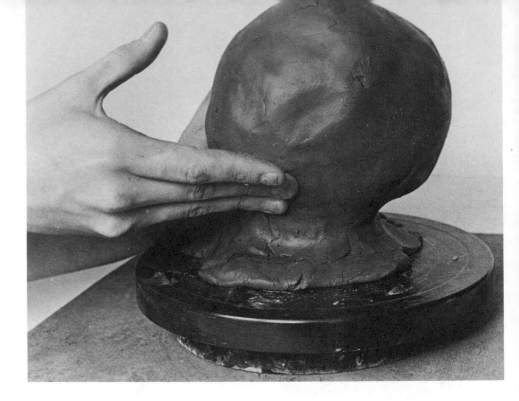

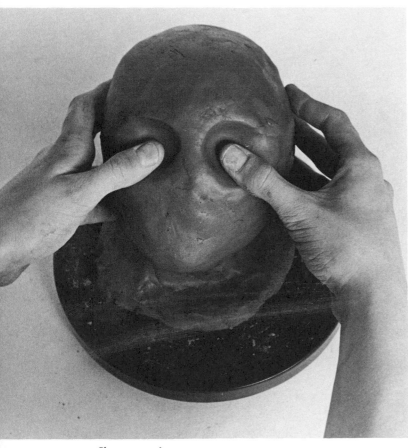

Shape eye sockets.

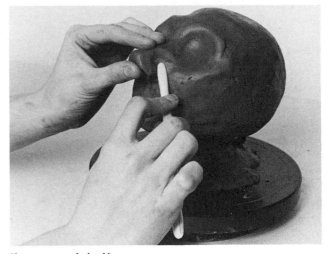

Shape nose and cheekbones.

3. Push the eye sockets in by moving your thumbs back and forth.
4. Poke, push, pull and model the nose, forehead and cheekbones. Exaggerate!
5. Shape the mouth, lips and jaw.
6. Moist clay can be added to the forehead, eyebrows, cheeks, nose and chin. Be sure not to trap air beneath the surface when you add clay. Smooth it carefully onto the clay head.

Shape mouth, lips and jaw.

Add eyes.

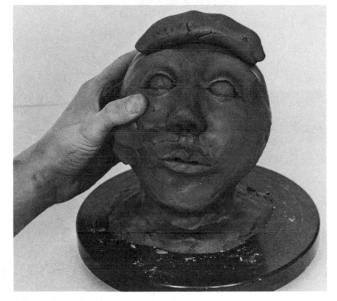

Adding clay to build up prominent features.

Step Four: **Form the eyes.**

1. Roll two tiny balls of the same size. Place them symmetrically in the two eye sockets. Score to secure.
2. Make two small slab "pockets" for the upper eyelids. Attach these to the eye sockets so that they overlap part of the eyeballs. Use the rounded edge of a clay tool to smooth and shape the upper lid. Add a lower lid if desired.

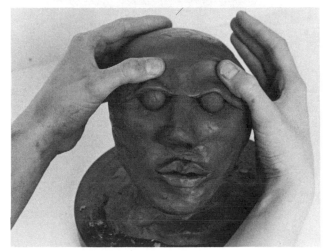

Add upper lids.

Step Five: **Form the ears.**

1. Look at the back of the clay head. Locate where the ears should be.
2. Use thumbs and clay tools to push, press, lift and model a thick clay ear from the head.
3. Shape ears from all sides and smooth.

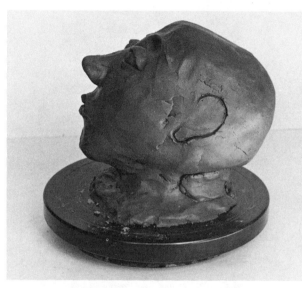

Locate ears.

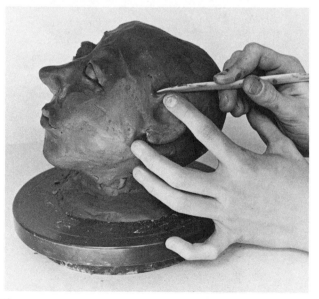

Shape ears.

It is the lack of features and expression on this face which makes it both disconcerting and mysterious. Detail, **Marble Figure,** *Greek, early Cycladic, plastiras type, circa 2700* B.C. *23″ × 5¼″ (59 × 13.5 cm). Courtesy Mead Art Museum, Amherst College, Amherst, Massachusetts. Gift of Mr. and Mrs. A. M. Adler.*

Though the artist has not included the actual flute, the style, position and expression of this bust make the flute seem to materialize before our eyes. **Virtuoso,** David Aronson. *Courtesty Pucker/Safrai Gallery, Boston, Massachusetts.*

The elongated neck, upturned chin, arched brows and high cheekbones help give this beautiful woman a regal manner. Detail, **Seated Navajo Woman,** R. C. Gorman. *Courtesy of the artist.*

Step Six: **Give your sculpture personality and expression.**

What is it that determines who your character is? What is it that makes your head come to life and assume a personality of its own? Consider the following:

Style: Terms such as *realistic, abstract, highly designed, exaggerated, simplified* or *understated* are used to describe style. What is the style of head that you are sculpting?

Position or Carriage: Is your character self-assured, nervous, dreamy, shy, friendly, a snob? The position or tilt of the head tells the viewer a great deal about your character. Look at the heads in this chapter. What strikes you about the position of each head? Assume the positions yourself. How do you feel?

Emotion or Expression: Look in the mirror or at each other and try to make faces that express the following emotions: joy, sorrow, anger, hate, love, pain. Notice the ways your facial features change as you change emotions. Exaggerate the emotion of your clay head by working with the slant of the eyebrows, the tilt of the mouth, the size of the nose, the opening of the eyes, the thrust of the chin and the hollows of the cheeks.

Step Seven: **Model the hairline.**

1. Look at the hairline of several individuals. Follow the hairline all around the head.
2. Find the hairline of your clay head.
3. Push with fingers, thumbs, and tools to lift the hairline all around. Try to make it stand up from the head.

Lift the hairline with thumbs and tools.

Step Eight: Style the hair.

Decide what style of hair your character will have. It can be long, short, curly, wavy, straight, thick, thin or braided. Is your character bald? Does your character have a receding hairline, beard, mustache or bushy eyebrows? Hair can be made from coils, slabs and balls of clay. Make strands of hair by squeezing clay through a screen or a garlic press. If you add on clay parts, they should be fairly thick. Carefully attach them by scoring. Thin and poorly-attached pieces of clay hair are the first parts to fall off during drying.

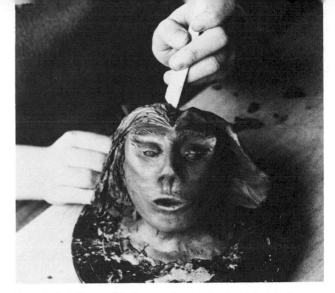

To make hair from a slab, be sure that the clay is thick. Join it securely to the head before texturing.

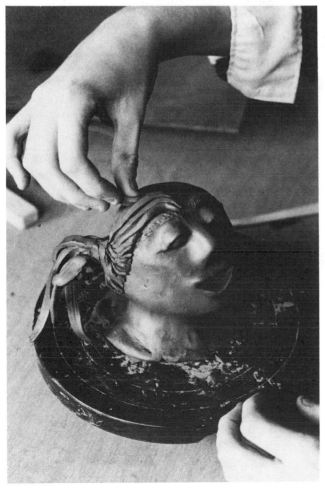

These strands of clay hair were sliced from a thick slab and applied to the clay in a whimsical manner.

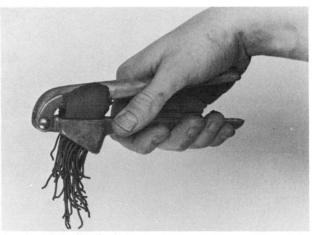

A garlic press makes clay hair.

Completed Head, Simone Topal, age 14.

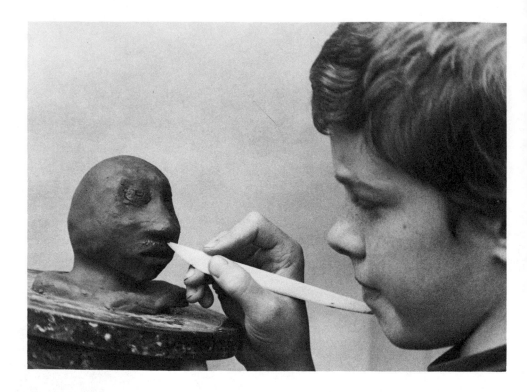

You can style some hair without adding clay.

Clay Head, Tracy Ahearn, grade 8.

Step Nine: **Store, finish and dry your sculpture.**

To store unfinished clay heads or faces, keep them moist. Drape them with a damp towel or cloth and enclose them in airtight containers or sealed plastic bags. See Appendix for more information.

When a clay head is finished, cut and shape the base of the neck so that the head is balanced and stands straight. Smooth the base.

Left uncovered, the outside of a clay head dries much faster than the inside. A clay head should dry slowly, under plastic, so that the clay can dry at a more uniform rate. Cracks will be less likely to occur and added pieces will be less likely to fall off.

This is a long-term project, requiring more than one session. For that reason it is important to wrap sculptures so they will stay moist while stored. See Appendix for instructions. Remember to put names on the outside of the plastic storage bags so that sculptures can be identified.

Clay Head, Seth Goldsmith, grade 6.

Clay Head, Roger Riel, grade 8.

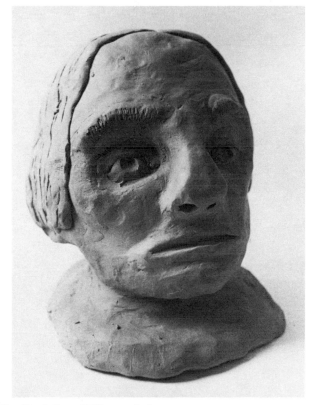

Clay Head, Steve Phillips, grade 8.

Clay Head, Ian Dell'Antonio, grade 8.

Summary of concepts in sculpting heads and faces

By modeling a freestanding head, sculpture students can see that the study of anatomy is an integral part of sculpting a realistic form. The subtle aspects of **style, position, carriage** and **expression** become tangible as students give shape and character to a clay face. By interpreting and exaggerating facial forms, students experience the complexity and rewards of the artistic process.

Contrasts in texture help make a strong composition in this figure sculpture. **Praying Nobleman,** Sumerian, *Mari, about 2600 B.C. Alabaster, 14"* *(36 cm). The Nelson–Atkins Museum of Art,* *Kansas City, Missouri (Nelson Fund).*

7

FIGURES

Figure sculptures, sculptures that represent people, have their own mystique. No matter how crude the form, there is something pleasing about a figure sculpture.

People in many cultures have believed that figure sculptures possess power. Images of warriors have been formed to increase chances of success in battle. Sculptors have made figures of full-breasted and full-bellied women to assure fertile land and abundant crops. In early times people created idealized images of the human form and worshipped them as gods and goddesses. Many civilizations have immortalized their heroes by erecting statues in their honor. To this day people continue to be fascinated by figure sculptures, creating them in a remarkable number of different media, styles and sizes. We follow in a time-honored tradition.

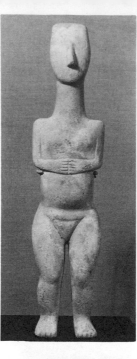

The straightforward position and the absence of gesture or action makes this figure quite thought-provoking and mysterious. Figures such as this ancient woman were believed to have been used as household deities until the owner's death. At that time they were buried in the owner's tomb. **Marble Figure,** *Greek, early Cycladic, plastiras type, circa 2700* B.C. *23″ × 5¼″ (59 × 13.5 cm). Courtesy Mead Art Museum, Amherst College, Amherst, Massachusetts. gift of Mr. and Mrs. A. M. Adler.*

This is one soldier from an army of 7,500 life-size clay soldiers and horses. This fantastic army, which was meant to serve the First Emperor Qin in his after-life, was buried over 2,000 years ago and was just recently unearthed. Each hollow figure was sculpted from clay coils, fired and brightly painted. The soldier's stance is believed to be a movement in taijiquan, the martial art of shadow-boxing. **Unarmed Soldier,** Chinese, *from the ancient capital city of Xi'an, circa 221* B.C. *Terra cotta with traces of paint, life-size. Courtesy Embassy of the People's Republic of China, Washington, D.C.*

Like sculpted animals, figure sculptures take on life and personality as they are modeled and positioned. By positioning a figure to emphasize an action, sculptors are able to illustrate situations and express emotions. Some preparation is needed to work with this concept.

The following body sculpting exercises enable students to experience the many challenges and potential problems of figure sculpting before working in clay. Students can sense the solutions in their own bodies. These exercises also help generate sculpture ideas.

Body Awareness Exercises: Students stand an arm's length apart. The teacher can model each position, pointing out the joints, the weight distribution and the proportions of one body part to another. Students imitate each position, becoming more aware of all the parts of the body and how they move.

Tiny, highly detailed and realistic sculptures sometimes show people working at a trade. Here we see a barrelmaker looking up from his work. His tools are carefully portrayed. **Barrelmaker at Work,** *artist unknown, Okimono, Japan, 19th century. Ivory, 2½″ × 2″ (6.5 × 5.3 cm). Courtesy George Walter Vincent Smith Art Museum, Springfield, Massachusetts.*

Body Sculpting: In body sculpting each person works with a partner and takes at least one turn being the sculptor and another being the sculpture. Sculptures go limp and allow sculptors to arrange them into dramatic positions. Positions can express emotions such as fear, anger, joy and hate, or concepts such as rebellion, shyness or hiding. Sculptors can try various levels such as lying down, sitting, bending, standing and stretching up. Sculptors should decide how to arrange every limb and joint.

1

2

3

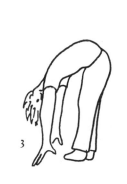

5

6

7

8

9

10

11

12

1. Length of body: Stretch up to the ceiling. Stand on tip-toes to become as tall as you can. Stretch every part of your body.
2. Neck joint: Turn your neck as far to the right as you can, then as far to the left as you can. Look up. Look down. Roll your neck around in a circle.
3. Waist joint: Bend at your waist. Try to touch the floor. Touch the fingertips of your right hand to your left toe, and vice versa. Look between your legs.
4. Waist joint: Stand up. Swing your arms to the right as far as they will go, then to the left. Feel your waist twist.
5. Shoulder joint: Stretch your arms out as far as they can go. Feel where your arms attach to your body at the shoulders. Rotate your arms.
6. Elbow joint, arm proportions: Bend your arms at the elbows. Touch your wrists to your shoulders. The distance between your wrist and elbow equals the distance between your elbow and shoulder.

7. Length of arm, wrist joint: Drop your arms down to your sides. Where do they touch? Did you realize that they were so long? Rotate your wrists.
8. Hip joints: Swing your leg up into the air. Where does it attach to the body? Swing your other leg, too.
9. Knee joint: Bend your leg at the knee, as far as you can. The distance between your hip and knee equals the distance between your knee and ankle. Rotate your ankles. Point your toes.
10. Weight shift: Stand with your legs spread apart. Bend your right knee. Feel the weight of your body shift. Now straighten your right knee and bend your left knee.
11. Sports pose: "On your mark. Get set." Try poses from different sports. Where is the weight of your body resting? Which limbs are doing the supporting?
12. Emotion: Get into a position that expresses an emotion such as joy, hate, sorrow or anger. Use standing, sitting and lying down positions. Where does the body weight lie? What characterizes the position?

Notice the graceful, curved position of this lovely little figure. Though the sculpture is delicate, the artist made it much sturdier by connecting all of the appendages to the main form. **Girl Arranging a Flower in her Hair,** *artist unknown, Bali. Wood, 6″ (15.2 cm). Courtesy of Flora W. Slonim.*

This cellist is entirely caught up in his playing. The sway of his body, his billowing sleeves, his closed eyes and his expressive hands communicate the impact and power of music. **Cellist,** David Aronson, 1969–1978. *Clay model, 14¼″ × 11½″ × 20¼″ (36.2 × 29.2 × 51.4 cm). Courtesy Pucker/Safrai Gallery, Boston, Massachusetts. Photograph by Barney Burstein.*

Action Quiz: One student at a time freezes in a position from a sport or an everyday activity. The rest of the class tries to guess what the student is doing. As each person takes a turn, consider whether a pose would be successful if modeled in clay. Point out where the weight of the body is resting.

When beginning a figure sculpture, remember that small figures are easier to model than big ones. Start small and work up to larger figures. Following are two approaches to sculpting figures. Students do not agree on which method is easiest or works best. Try both methods and experiment.

In this figure, the Eskimo sculptor has captured a fleeting moment. This is the instant before the blow, when all of the fisherman's energy, concentration and skill are poised to act. The simplified forms accentuate the position and emotional impact of this sculpture. Students can try this position and notice where their energy is concentrated. **Fisherman,** Ryitook. *Carved soapstone. Courtesy Pucker/Safrai Gallery, Boston, Massachusetts. Photograph by George Wasquez.*

Figures from coils and balls

Materials: Small balls of moist clay, pointed sticks or clay tools.

Directions:
1. Wedge a ball of clay and divide it into three pieces — small, medium and large. Roll a ball from the small piece. From the larger pieces roll two coils about as thick as your thumb.
2. Press the ball and two coils together to make a person. The ball can become a head, and the two coils can become the arms and legs.

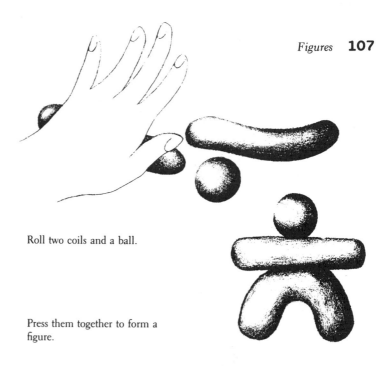

Roll two coils and a ball.

Press them together to form a figure.

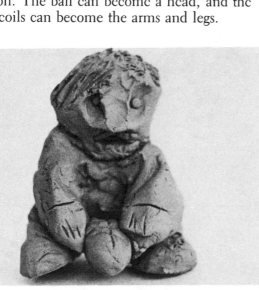

Clay Figure Holding Football, student, age 5.

Sitting Figure, student, age 10.

Boy Reading, Stephen Holsten, age 10.

3. Smooth all the parts together until you cannot tell where they were joined. Shape the person as you go. Make the upper arms and thighs thicker than the forearms and lower legs. Try not to make the arms or legs too skinny. They tend to break off if they are too long and thin. If a part does break off, reshape it and attach it securely. Use a fresh ball of clay if your first ball has dried out.

4. Carefully bend your figure into a position. Rejoin any parts that separate. Try the position yourself to see where the body weight is resting. Experiment with several positions.

Join the parts together.

Reinforce supporting parts.

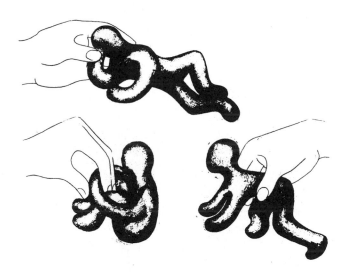

Give the figure a position.

Add texture and details.

Hockey Player, Seljuk Burk, age 10.

5. Be sure that your sculpture is sturdy. You may want to review this in Chapter Three. Add extra clay to supporting parts. Connect appendages to the body for added support and smooth the entire sculpture.

6. Add details, features and textures with fingers or by using a clay tool. Add only one or two details to make the effect more dramatic.

7. Refine your sculpture. Try to look at your figure as a shape in space. You are finished when your sculpture is sturdy and looks unified from all points of view.

Modeling figures

Materials: Moist clay (small balls), pointed sticks, pencils or clay tools.

Directions:
1. Wedge a ball of clay and roll it to the shape of a very thick sausage.
2. Gently squeeze a neck a little way in from the end of the sausage shape. Then form the head. Don't let the neck get too thin!
3. Use a sharp tool to cut slits for the arms and legs.
4. Shape all the body parts.
5. Position and complete your figure according to previous directions, adding one or two textures or details.

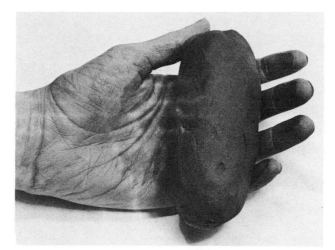

Roll a fat sausage.

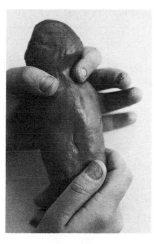

Squeeze the neck.

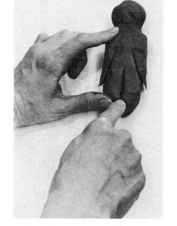

Cut slits.

Separate the appendages.

Shape the appendages.

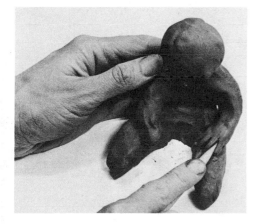

Add detail.

Finished figure.

Looking at this sculpture we sense a parent's pride in an infant. The baby reaches out and looks up as if to greet the world. The parent's proud gaze centers on the baby. **Immortality,** Victor Salmones. *Bronze, 36″ (91.4 cm). Gallery Victor, Acapulco, Mexico. Photograph courtesy of the artist.*

Figures and scenes

As the children finish a figure sculpture, they can add to it by putting another figure in some relationship to the first one. They can add other forms and details, or place figures in a setting with landscape materials such as shells, rocks, grasses or furniture.

"Person and animal" usually is a successful theme for a combination sculpture. Children also enjoy sculpting from such themes as "Father and Child," "Mother and Child," or "My Friend and I." They enjoy recreating scenes from daily life, episodes from books and habitats that they have studied.

In medieval times falconing was a sport of kings. Here a king's falconer seems to be preparing a bird for the hunt. **Falconer,** *anonymous, French, 15th century. Polychromed wood, 26″ × 5¾″ (66 × 14.6 cm). Courtesy Smith College Museum of Art, Northampton, Massachusetts.*

Combine individual sculptures into one larger piece for a very workable small group project. **Three Women Reading on a Park Bench,** students, age 11.

In this sculpture the artist shows that humans can assume characteristics similar to those of animals. Here the man has an "owl-like" build, position and manner. His body is massive, his head small and facing forward. Man and owl seem secure and at peace with one another. Both seem to be sitting back, waiting and watching. **Seated Man with Owl,** Leonard Baskin, 1959. *Cherry wood, 30″ × 16¹⁵⁄₁₆″ × 17¾″ (76.2 × 40.7 × 45.1 cm). Courtesy Smith College Museum of Art, Northampton, Massachusetts.*

The friendly yet respectful relationship between this man and bird differs from the relationship in the other sculpture examples. Notice the tilt of the man's and the bird's heads. Where are they looking? Note the many intricately carved designs and textures on this precisely and beautifully carved sculpture. **Bird Tamer,** Shinji, *Okimono, Japan, 19th century. Ivory, 3⅛″ × 2¼″ (8 × 7 cm). Courtesy George Walter Vincent Smith Art Museum, Springfield, Massachusetts.*

This delicately carved miniature scene shows details of Eskimo life. We see igloos, household creatures, fresh-caught seals lashed onto a sled and a polar bear hide curing on the igloo's roof. **Igloo Composition,** Ipellie Oshoweetok. *Soapstone, length 17″ (36.2 cm). Courtesy Pucker/Safrai Gallery, Boston, Massachusetts.*

Two or more clay forms can be positioned in an unlimited number of combinations. Sculpting can be easier when you connect separate forms. One form can balance and support another.

Students should keep one form moist under plastic while working on the other. Use the composition section in Chapter Three as a reference to make an arrangement that shows the relationship between the figure and the animal. Try several arrangements before carefully joining the two forms. To add stability to a combination sculpture, score figures, animals and other forms onto a thick clay slab base.

Summary of figure sculpture concepts

With practice at making figure sculptures, students reinforce their understanding of **proportion, texture, mass** and **point of view**. They can come to understand **weight distribution** and learn to **connect forms** or **reinforce** them with extra clay for sturdiness. Children can see that **use of one or two details** may give a sculpture greater impact than would many details. Creation of a group scene can help students learn to work together.

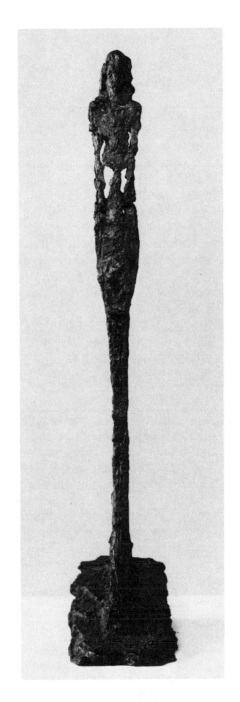

In contrast to smooth-surfaced figure sculptures, Giacometti's figures are characterized by rough surfaces. The roughness enhances the artist's evocative designs. **Femme debout,** Giacometti, *circa* 1952. *Bronze, 20¼" × 3¾" × 6¾" (50.5 × 9.5 × 17 cm). Courtesy Galerie Maeght, New York.*

8

IMPROVING SCULPTURES

Students can improve their sculptures if they pause to get a fresh view of their work. Sometimes children can lose sight of the overall form of their sculpture when they concentrate too much on the one area they are sculpting. It is also helpful for an entire class to pause and get a new perspective by examining and discussing the group's various solutions to sculpture problems. This evaluating process is known as a **critique.**

A critique is not simply criticism; it is evaluation with a critical eye, looking for good points and weak points. A critique should help students become aware of what they have accomplished and should help them decide how to proceed from this point. A critique may focus on design, technique or craft skills.

Leading a group critique

It is important for each student to come away from a critique feeling positive about some aspect of his or her work. For this reason it is best to make and abide by a rule that comments about any work of art should be made only in positive or helpful ways. The group can point out aspects of sculptures that worked *well*. Students are quick to notice the aspects of their own sculptures that need more work.

Critiques should be held at various times during the sculpting process. They are perhaps most valuable when work is in process. The critique time is an exciting, open time to help students realize what is special about their sculptures. This will

help them capitalize on the unique qualities of their sculpture. It is a time to make changes and a time to reinforce skills and concepts. It is also a time to catch problems before it is too late to fix them.

Critiques can be done individually, in small groups or with an entire class. They need not be formal, long or tedious. Often a sentence or two will do. Ask individuals to step back a few feet to look at what is happening in their sculptures. This is a simple and effective way of critiquing a sculpture. Just a few feet of distance helps students see their sculptures in a more objective way. Be sure to turn the sculpture as you look at it with the student, to see it from many points of view.

For example, if a student has pulled four sturdy protuberances that face in different directions, the student should decide whether or not to emphasize one direction to create a center of interest. The student might prefer to contrast areas by using texture. A critique is a good time to suggest that students strengthen small pieces by thickening them with more clay or by connecting them to another form.

Take a few minutes during the middle of a work period so students can walk around the room and look at each other's work. This is another way to let them step back from their own sculpting. Children quickly see how their classmates have solved problems similar to their own. Students should look for such qualities as sturdy positions or textures that follow the form of the sculpture. This helps to focus students' attention on sculpture problems and solutions rather than on liking or disliking the sculpture they see.

In this humorous sculpture, the figures are simplified to geometric shapes. They face forward, with no gestures or limbs. Features are missing, too, save for two eyes on top of the shorter figure's head. Yet the sculpture says much about the stereotyped image of the stately, shapely mother and her chubby, short daughter, or is it the tall shapely daughter and her chubby short mother? **Daughter and Mother (Fille et Mère),** Max Ernst, 1959. *Bronze, 17⅝″ × 10⅝″ × 11¾″ (44.6 × 26.9 × 28.8 cm). Courtesy Hirshhorn Museum and Sculpture Garden, Smithsonian Institution, Washington, D.C. © Estate of Max Ernst.*

Short group meetings are good because they reach all students in a short time. Limit the time to no more than five or ten minutes, especially for young children. This helps stave off restlessness. To ensure objectivity, the group should not know which student made which sculpture. Focus on one of two skills or concepts — the ones that students have understood and used well or the ones that they find difficult.

A critique can focus on sculptures that are alike in some way. For example, make groups of the sculptures that use space particularly well, sculptures that are smooth and well finished, sculptures that have unique connections between forms or sculptures with unusual protuberances. In looking at the work of an entire class, groupings will become evident. Students can discover what the sculptures in each group have in common.

Be sensitive to the youngsters who seem to have difficulty or who are dissatisfied with their work. Try to use their sculptures as examples to point out something that worked well — a well-joined part, an interesting texture, a repetition of shape or a good use of space. By doing this, teachers help children see their work in a new way. Usually those students will feel a new confidence and will return to their sculpting with a different attitude.

Discussion topics

The following discussion topics and questions are a beginning point for evaluating on-going work, finished work or sculptures by noted artists. Use sculpture vocabulary and concepts as much as possible in discussion and critiques. Don't try to cover everything at once or students will be overwhelmed. Choose one topic or question as a focus.

What is the sculpture's message?

Does the sculpture tell you something about the way people live: their traditions, beliefs, family structure or work life? Is it intended to immortalize a god or person? Does it commemorate a historical event or act as a symbol for a people, country, religion or organization? Is it trying to convey a political message? Does it capture a moment or a vision of beauty for all time? Does the sculpture make

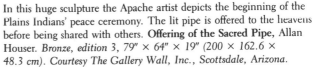

In this huge sculpture the Apache artist depicts the beginning of the Plains Indians' peace ceremony. The lit pipe is offered to the heavens before being shared with others. **Offering of the Sacred Pipe,** Allan Houser. *Bronze, edition 3, 79″ × 64″ × 19″ (200 × 162.6 × 48.3 cm). Courtesy The Gallery Wall, Inc., Scottsdale, Arizona.*

you look at forms, materials and space in a new way? Is the sculpture designed to give definition and distinction to a particular space, outdoors or indoors? For adults or children? Who is the audience meant to be?

How was the sculpture made?

What materials were used? What techniques? Is the sculpture freestanding or in relief? Is the sculpture sturdy? What makes it so? Do you think an armature was used? Why? Can you tell where the parts were joined?

Is the sculpture made well?

Did the artist carefully finish this work of art? Is it well crafted? Do all the parts of the sculpture work together to create a unified whole?

How would you describe the shapes in the sculpture?

Are they light or heavy? Organic or geometric? Regular or irregular? Angular or curved? Open or closed? Separate or connected?

How is the sculpture organized?

Are there repetitions of forms and spaces to give unity and rhythm to the sculpture? Are there contrasting areas, textures or forms to add interest and excitement? Does the sculpture seem to move in a particular direction (horizontal, vertical, diagonal, curving)? Is it organized on the basis of a growth pattern (spiral, concentric, branching)? Are there any progressions (small to large, rough to smooth, curves to angles)? Where would you place the center of interest? Why?

What effects does the sculpture have on you?

How does the sculpture make you feel? Scared? Protected? Amused? Does the sculpture seem friendly, inviting, angry or repelling? Why? Can you associate the sculpture with an emotion such as love, hate, pain, sorrow or joy? Do you associate the sculpture with something in nature or in the human-made world?

Discussions challenge students to look, to make comparisons, to relate forms to personal experiences. Students learn to see and think about the artistic expressions of people from different cultures and to verbalize their findings. This is an important way of understanding the artistic process and product. Discussions help students place artwork within the larger framework of human experience.

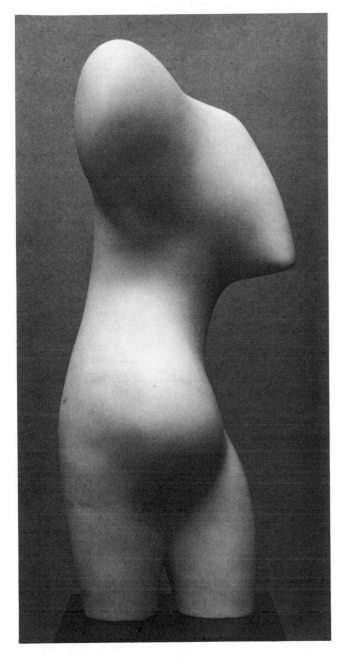

A smoothly-polished surface helps unify the curved forms in this sculpture. The contrast of the sharp black base lends additional impact. **Torso,** Jean (Hans) Arp, 1953. *White marble on black stone, 31⅜" (80.6 cm). Courtesy Smith College Museum of Art, Northampton, Massachusetts. Gift of Mr. and Mrs. Ralph Colin, 1956.*

9

FINISHING AND DISPLAYING SCULPTURE

When clay sculptures have been completed, ask students to sign their names on the bottom of each clay piece using a pencil. Remind students to write lightly and legibly. Young children tend to write very big and to press too hard, so it is preferable to have the teacher write young children's names on the bottom of the clay sculptures as they are collected. At this time the teacher can check each sculpture to see whether or not it will survive the drying process, and can ask students to make repairs if necessary.

Drying and firing

Store the work of each class out of reach on a separate board or shelf. This will make it easier to identify work later. Allow sculptures to dry slowly. This prevents smaller parts from drying out too fast and cracking off from larger parts. Dry sculptures under loosely fitting, open plastic bags to slow down and even out the drying process. If left in such a state for several hours or overnight, sculptures soon will be leather hard. When sculptures are leather hard they can be hollowed out, sanded, smoothed, carved and refined. Hollowing helps the piece dry at an even rate and reduces the possibility of there being air bubbles trapped in the clay. Bubbles would cause the piece to explode when fired in the kiln.

At the leather hard stage, additional pieces may be added by scoring. Younger children are apt to destroy their sculptures if they continue work at this stage; older children have the patience and control to work gently and carefully. They often find this stage of sculpting most rewarding.

This is a bisqued sculpture. **Greek Deity,** Kaori Shioti, age 10. Photograph by Valerie Kemp.

Eagle Cup, Raul Perez, age 17.

Greenware

Most sculptures take about a week to dry out. At this time they will feel warm and dry to the touch. Dry sculptures are quite vulnerable, so it is especially important to keep them away from curious hands. Dry unfired clay is known as **greenware** and is ready to be bisque-fired in the kiln.

A kiln is an oven that has extremely thick, fire-resistant insulation and is able to reach very high temperatures. Some kilns fire only low-fire clay. Others reach higher temperatures and are able to fire high-fire clay. A kiln should be located out of the way, far enough from walls to allow free air circulation. A peephole, a pyrometer to indicate temperature, and an automatic shut-off are features to look for when choosing a kiln. If you cannot purchase a kiln, many local potters will fire sculptures for a small fee.

Do not be discouraged if you do not have access to a kiln. Clay can simply be left unfired. Students will have experienced all the benefits of completing a sculpture. Dried sculptures can be finished using any of the ways suggested in this chapter's section on glazing without firing.

There are several self-hardening clays and clays that can be baked in the oven. Consult your local art store for details. Keep in mind that most of the exercises in this book can also be done with Playdough or Plasticene.

Bisque firing

Clay becomes harder and more durable when fired in a kiln under very high heat, a process that fuses the chemicals in the clay. After firing, clay will not return to its moist, muddy state when placed in water.

The first firing is called a bisque firing. No glaze is involved. Sculptures without glaze will not fuse together, so many clay pieces can be fired at the same time. They should be carefully placed in the kiln close to one another. They may also be gently stacked on top of one another. Heavier sculptures should be on the bottom. Watch out for sculptures with delicate protuberances. They break easily.

Bisque firings take almost a day because the temperature in the kiln must be brought up slowly to remove any remaining moisture. It is wise to check on the kiln while it is firing. The kiln must then be allowed to cool overnight before it is opened, or the sculptures may cool too fast and crack.

Occasionally small pieces of clay break. If both pieces are fired, they can be glued with white glue. They cannot go through a glaze firing after they have been glued, however.

Glazing

A glaze is a coating that enables pots to retain liquids. Glazes embellish the surface of the clay. Glazes are not a necessity for sculpture, however. A shiny coating and color added to bisqued clay can change the look of a sculpture dramatically in positive and negative ways. Care must be taken not to overpower the sculpture with colors and textures that detract from the form of the sculpture itself. Bisqued sculptures often are effective without any kind of coating.

Glazed relief sculpture. **Cityscape** by Todd Kastner, age 11.

Bisqued relief sculpture.

A display can include natural materials.

Lady drinking hot soup, eating popcorn while watching TV in bed by Hilary Sweeny, age 8.

A matte glaze gives this sculpted vase a smooth, colorful look without the gloss of a standard glaze. **Vase**, Shildialv. 9″ (22.9 cm). Collection of Carolyn and Steven Dashef.

Glazing for firing

Glaze comes in a powder form (which you can mix according to directions) or in liquid form. There are low-fire and high-fire glazes which correspond to low-fire and high-fire clay. It is safest to apply clear glaze or one solid color to the entire bisqued sculpture. Apply two or three even coats of glaze in opposite directions. The number of coats needed depends on the thickness of the glaze.

For safety, be sure to use lead-free glazes. Always wear a respirator or a similar high-quality breathing filter when mixing powdered glazes.

Before applying glaze, dampen the bottom of the sculpture to prevent glaze from sticking there. The bottom of each clay piece must be left unglazed so that the sculpture does not become fused to the kiln. At the bottom of the sculpture dampen about ¼ inch or ⅔ centimeters and leave it unglazed as well. This prevents glaze from dripping down and fusing the sculpture to the floor or shelf of the kiln.

Glazed sculptures must be fired again to finish the glaze. Because glazed pieces can fuse together easily if they touch, they must be separated in the kiln. Small trivets can be used to elevate sculptures in the kiln to prevent sticking. Glazed sculptures must be fired to a higher temperature than in bisquing. The higher temperature causes the glass particles in the glaze to fuse to the clay. In a glaze firing the kiln can be turned to high right away because the moisture has already been removed during the bisque firing. The glaze firing is shorter.

Another option in glazing is to use an underglaze/overglaze combination. Underglazes come in an array of colors, just like paint, and are applied to the clay. Once the underglaze is dry, spread an even layer of clear overglaze on the entire sculpture, except the bottom. Then fire the sculpture. The result is a shiny, multicolored sculpture. This method works best with students who have enough physical control to paint tiny details. Underglazes also come in pencil, crayon, and watercolor forms. These are easier to control.

Glazing without firing

Sculptures do not need to be glazed to have a shiny and colorful finish. There are many simpler, cheaper and quicker methods. Because clay is very absorbant, plan to apply more than one coat.

Clear shellac acts as a glaze. Although it is not very attractive over white clay, it deepens the color of red clay and gives the sculpture a shiny coating. Shellac thinner must be used to clean the brushes. **Shellac and shellac thinner must be used in a well-ventilated space because the fumes are potentially hazardous.**

These masks were finished with brightly colored acrylic paint. **Clay Masks,** children ages 6 and 7.

Slate and concrete sealer, available at hardware stores, can be used in much the same way as shellac. Use this sealer directly from the can to add a clear, shiny finish, or mix it with oil paint to add color. **Lacquer thinner is required to rinse brushes. It is potentially hazardous and should be used only in a well-ventilated area.** Slate and concrete sealer will make the sculptures waterproof if applied generously and thoroughly.

A safe and easy alternative is clear, glossy acrylic polymer medium. This can be used just as shellac is used. Unlike shellac, however, it does not deepen the color of the clay. Acrylic polymer medium works well over white clay. If a color is desired, mix a few drops of acrylic paint into the medium. Dark colors such as Prussian or navy blue, wine or raw umber help to bring out textures. Thin the mixture with a little water to make it flow more easily. This method has the advantage that brushes can be washed out with water and there are no hazardous fumes.

Sculptures may be painted in detail with acrylic paints, then covered with clear acrylic polymer medium. The result resembles the underglaze/overglaze technique. To achieve a similar effect, decorate sculptures with poster paints, then coat them with clear shellac or varnish and allow them to dry thoroughly.

Sometimes gold or silver spray paint can be used to achieve unusual effects. Undoubtedly you can discover other successful finishes.

Two coats of clear shellac were applied to this relief sculpture. **Scene from Singapore,** Guek-Yang Seow.

Displaying

Before sculptures go home, they should be shared or displayed. Displays are terrific confidence builders. They reward the creator and show that good work is valued.

Sculptures have a more professional look when they are displayed in a manner that effectively shows them. Displays can be made quickly and easily from many available materials. Temporary displays can be set up for a quick look at on-going work.

Perhaps the easiest way to display sculptures is to place them on construction paper that is cut to size. Sculptures may be arranged on wooden blocks or planks. Natural materials such as an unusual piece of driftwood, marsh grass, cattails, dried flowers, shells, sea grass, ferns, plants or large rocks can provide a setting for a display. Try draping a box with a solid color cloth that contrasts with the color of the sculptures. Spray-painted boxes make dramatic display cases, too.

The title of each sculpture and the name of the sculptor are important parts of the display. Students should print or write their names and titles clearly with a black marker or ballpoint pen. Neatly fold a small white piece of paper in half to make a simple name card that will stand.

Children are quite inventive in building pedestals, in grouping sculptures and in dreaming up titles for their completed works. When they set up and critique their own displays, with the aid and encouragement of a teacher, they become aware of display as an art in itself.

Figure sculptures on display by children ages 10 and 11.

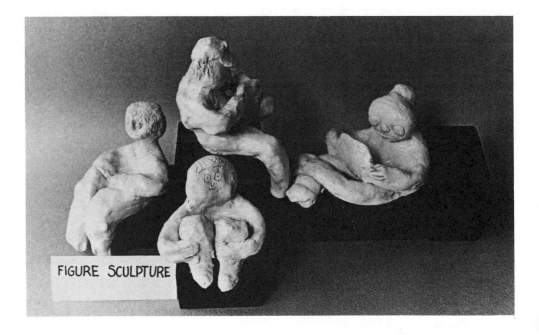

FIGURE SCULPTURE

APPENDIX

Purchasing clay

Clay can be purchased in most local art stores and from potters living in your area. Look up pottery-making supplies in your telephone book. Clay comes in two forms, as a powder to which water must be added, or as moist clay that is ready for use. Clay is relatively inexpensive and can be used over and over again before it is fired.

For regular classroom use buy low-fire clay, which comes in red, gray, buff or white. It can be fired in a kiln or left in the air to dry. There are several oven-fire clays on the market that can be baked in an oven at about 250 degrees Fahrenheit. There are self-hardening clays, as well.

Storing clay

To keep unfinished sculptures workable for several days or overnight, place a moist, but not soaking wet, rag or paper towel over the sculpture. Then place the sculpture in an airtight container such as a plastic bag, and seal it with a wire twist. Store unfinished sculptures on a board for easier handling. Sculptures may be stored individually or as a group. To protect many sculptures, store them on one big board, drape them with damp towels or rags and cover them with a large plastic garbage bag.

Store large quantities of clay for a long time in a plastic garbage can with a tight-fitting lid, in a double layer of plastic bags or in a ceramic crock.

Reclaiming clay

If clay has dried out simply crack it up into small pieces with a hammer or mallet, put it back into an airtight container, add a little water and let it sit for a day or two. Then wedge it and work it until the consistency feels right (see Chapter One). Children love to break up clay with a hammer or mallet, and it is an excellent way to learn about the nature of clay. Take safety precautions by placing the clay in a thick bag before breaking it. This will prevent the pieces from flying.

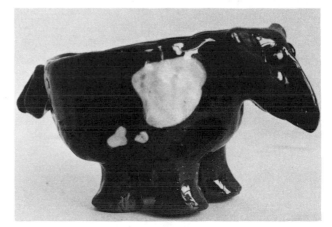

White and black underglazes were painted on the bisqued sculpture and allowed to dry. An overglaze was applied and the piece was re-fired. **Cow Pot** by the author, 1980. 3″ (7.6 cm).

GLOSSARY

Abstract A form that has been simplified or geometrized.

Additive Process An approach to sculpting; joining pieces to create a whole.

Armature An inner support structure for sculpture; usually made of wire, newspaper or cardboard.

Art Concepts Line, shape, texture, form, color and value.

Art Media The materials from which artwork is fashioned; in sculpture, often clay, wood, stone, wire, plaster or metal. Singular: **Medium.**

Bisque Clay that has been fired once at a low temperature; or unglazed, fired pieces of clay. Also used as a verb.

Clay Sketch A clay form that has been modeled quickly for the purpose of practicing a technique or trying an idea.

Coil A long clay form that looks like a snake. Coiling is an ancient technique used to make large pots and sculptures.

Composition The arrangement of forms in a work of art.

Design Principles Balance, movement, repetition, emphasis, contrast, and unity.

Form A shape that has length, width and depth.

Freestanding Modeled in the round and self supporting. A freestanding sculpture is not attached to a background, as a relief sculpture would be.

Geometric Of or relating to forms that are precise and regular, based on geometric structures such as cones, cubes, spheres, pyramids and cylinders.

Glaze A coating, applied to clay, that fuses and turns to glass when fired in a kiln under very high temperatures.

Greenware   Dry clay pots or sculptures that are ready for firing; dry, unfired clay.

Hollowing Out   Removing clay from the inside of a solid form to make the clay walls thinner, less apt to crack, and to make the sculpture lighter.

Intaglio   Line designs etched into a surface.

In the Round   Not attached to a background; not in relief; a sculpture in which all parts are visible except the bottom.

Kiln   A furnace or oven built of heat resistant materials for firing pottery or sculpture.

Leather Hard   Clay that has hardened, but is still cool and moist to the touch, like leather. Clay that is still soft enough to carve or to join by scoring.

Model   To form clay parts by gently working and manipulating the clay.

Mass   A shape that has length, width and depth.

Negative Shape   Areas or spaces around and between the solid forms of a sculpture.

Nonobjective   A form that is nonrepresentational.

Organic Shape   Free form; a form which is irregular, usually curvilinear, and is suggestive of forms in nature.

Positive Shapes   The solid parts of a sculpture.

Protuberance   A part that juts out into space.

Realistic   A form that is true to life.

Relief   Sculpture in which figures or forms project from a flat surface; compare with freestanding sculpture, which has forms modeled in the round.

Scoring   A technique for attaching two clay pieces together. The surfaces to be joined are scratched, covered with slip and firmly pressed together.

Sculpting   The art and craft of creating forms and arranging them in space.

Slab   A large flat piece of clay formed by rolling or throwing.

Slip   Clay watered down to the consistency of sour cream or soft butter.

Sturdy Form   A well-joined, self-supporting form that will survive drying and firing without breaking.

Subtractive Process   In sculpting, removing pieces from a solid form by carving away.

Texture   The quality of a surface; its roughness or smoothness.

Viewpoint   The position from which an object is observed.

Wedging   A preparatory process to remove air bubbles and to even the consistency of clay.

BIBLIOGRAPHY

Berensohn, Paulus. *Finding One's Way with Clay.* New York: Simon and Schuster, 1972.

Brommer, Gerald F. *Discovering Art History.* Worcester, MA: Davis Publications, Inc., 1981.

Cherry, Clare. *Creative Art for the Developing Child.* Belmont, CA: Pitman Learning, Inc., 1972.

Gatto, Joseph, Albert W. Porter, and Jack Selleck. *Exploring Visual Design.* Worcester, MA: Davis Publications, Inc., 1978

Horowitz, Elinor Lander. A *Child's Garden of Sculpture.* Washington, D.C.: Washingtonian Books, 1976. Out of print.

Janson, H. W. *History of Art.* Englewood, NJ: Prentice Hall, Inc., and New York: Harry Abrams, Inc., 1977.

Moore, Lamont. *The Sculptured Image.* New York: Franklin Watts, Inc., 1967. Out of print.

Paine, Roberta M. *Looking at Sculpture.* New York: Lothrop, Lee and Shepard Co., 1968. Out of print.

Priolo, Joan, and Anthony Priolo. *Ceramics by Coil and Slab.* New York: Sterling Publishing Co., Inc., 1979.

Read, Herbert. A *Concise History of Modern Sculpture.* New York: Oxford University Press, 1964.

Röttger, Ernst. *Creative Clay Design.* New York: Van Nostrand Reinhold, 1962. Out of print.

Sapiro, Maurice. *Clay: Hand Building Techniques.* Worcester, MA: Davis Publications, Inc., 1979.

Speight, Charlotte F. *Hands in Clay.* Sherman Oaks, CA: Alfred Publishing Co., Inc., 1979.

Townley, Mary Ross. *Another Look.* Menlo Park, CA: Addison-Wesley Publishing Co., 1978.

Wachowiak, Frank. *Emphasis Art: A Qualitative Art Program for the Elementary School.* 3rd ed. New York: Thomas Y. Crowell Co., 1977.

Index